Professor T. David Gordon is a gifted  teacher. His new book provides five ver help the believer to understand and app living. I am glad to see this book in print and commend seminarians, and church leaders who wish to deepen their knowledge of Christian faith and practice.

—**John Jefferson Davis**, Senior Professor of Systematic Theology and Christian Ethics, Gordon-Conwell Theological Seminary

Choose Better is a gift to the individual Christian and the church community at large. T. David Gordon has provided an accessible and applicable model for Christian decision-making. Much of the literature on ethical systems and models for choice-making are helpful to the academy but leave laypeople scratching their heads as to how to apply them in real life. Not so with *Choose Better*! This is a fabulous contribution to the field of ethics and an invaluable resource to professors and pastors alike.

—**Evan Lenow**, Author, *Ethics as Worship*

To my knowledge, this book is without equal as an explanation of the God-given tools in Scripture that help people to make good and better choices. I have taught these tools to my congregation, and I have used them when helping people make serious choices. God has used Dr. Gordon to explain these tools in a thoughtful and practical way that should be extremely helpful to thinking Christians everywhere. One good biblical idea can transform a life, but in this book there are five great biblical ideas that have transformed my life and my ministry. May God help us all to make better biblically informed choices with this book.

—**Stephen Migotsky**, Pastor, Jaffrey Presbyterian Church, Jaffrey, New Hampshire

My first exposure to Dr. Gordon's five models was in the late 1990s when he taught the material in adult Sunday school in the church

I planted, Amoskeag Presbyterian Church. I was impressed with the biblical breadth of his ethical proposal. The Reformed find an emphasis on the law to be a refreshingly concrete guide to the Christian life—but it is not the only guide. Gordon's five models capture the nuances of biblical ethics and thus provide a significant aid to Christian pilgrims.

—**Gregory Edward Reynolds**, Author; Editor, *Ordained Servant*

B. B. Warfield wrote that next to our longing to be *in* Christ is our longing to be *like* Christ. This pithy expression regarding the imitation of Christ is one of the ethical models that T. David Gordon explores in *Choose Better*. Additional models are opened to us by Dr. Gordon, who provides what every valuable teacher offers: scope. What was previously overlooked is now placed before our eyes to appreciate for its spiritual worth. This is such an important corrective for our dangerous naivete relating to spiritual warfare, and it is medicinal for anemic hearts that have shunned Lady Wisdom's healing embrace. For all who want a "knowledge of the truth, which accords with godliness," I cannot think of a better place to start than this compact little gem.

—**A. Craig Troxel**, Professor of Practical Theology, Westminster Seminary California

In choosing to read *Choose Better*, you are making an excellent choice toward growing in both your desire and your ability to live well before God and others. Asking better questions leads to discovering better answers, and so the five models in *Choose Better* bring the whole counsel of God to bear on ethics, leading beyond good decisions to better decisions.

—**Lee F. Veazey**, Pastor, Grace and Peace Presbyterian Church, Bellevue, Kentucky

CH(((OO))SE BETTER

CH◎◎SE
BETTER

FIVE BIBLICAL MODELS
FOR MAKING
ETHICAL DECISIONS

T. DAVID GORDON

PUBLISHING
P.O. BOX 817 • PHILLIPSBURG • NEW JERSEY 08865-0817

Scripture quotations are from the ESV® Bible (The Holy Bible, English Standard Version®), copyright © 2001 by Crossway, a publishing ministry of Good News Publishers. Used by permission. All rights reserved.

Italics within Scripture quotations indicate emphasis added.

Scripture quotations from the New Testament use the ESV's alternate, footnoted translation of *adelphoi* ("brothers and sisters").

Printed in the United States of America

Library of Congress Cataloging-in-Publication Data

Names: Gordon, T. David, 1954- author.
Title: Choose better : five biblical models for making ethical decisions / T. David Gordon.
Description: Phillipsburg, New Jersey : P&R Publishing, [2024] | Summary: "When trying to make good choices, how do we know what is best? Historically, Christians have emphasized five different ways of making ethical decisions. Gordon explains the strengths and weaknesses of each"-- Provided by publisher.
Identifiers: LCCN 2023048148 | ISBN 9781629952345 (paperback) | ISBN 9781629952352 (epub)
Subjects: LCSH: Decision making--Religious aspects. | Choice (Psychology)--Religious aspects. | Conduct of life.
Classification: LCC BL629.5.D43 G673 2024 | DDC 241.5--dc23/eng/20231213
LC record available at https://lccn.loc.gov/2023048148

This book is dedicated to the memory of my parents,

John and Trudy Gordon,

whose examples of Christian virtue we took for granted
when we were young children but admired sincerely
and gratefully as we matured.

CONTENTS

PREFACE

If you ask most people what "ethics" is about, they will say that it is about distinguishing right from wrong, and there is surely some truth to this answer. Unfortunately, the answer is also limiting and implies that "ethics" is merely or primarily a matter of getting the right answer to some specific question about a moral choice. Ethics is much more comprehensive than this, however. Ethics is the study of how to live and how to live well. From the Greeks, we derive the term *axiology*, which means the study of what is worthy or worthwhile, presumably in all of life's endeavors (thus including what we might call *aesthetics* or labor-leisure issues in the field of what we might call *ethics*).

Human Choices in Light of Human Nature

Within a theistic framework, ethics is about living as God our Maker intended us to live. The ethical task is to think, in a disciplined and faithful way, about human *choices* in light of human nature, the human condition, human potential, and the divine creational mandate for humans. In this broader sense, every decision we make in life is "ethical"; it either contributes to or detracts from human life as God created it. "Business ethics," by such an understanding, comprehends far more than issues of ethical compromise or bookkeeping shenanigans—it also includes thinking about labor itself, commerce itself, and economics itself (not to mention mass consumerism), within a genuinely theistic framework, and considering how we ought to set about achieving God's purposes for labor, society, and economics.

To think about human choices in terms of human nature, for instance, we immediately recognize that thinking about choices is *itself* a reflection of human nature. The other creatures function primarily, though not exclusively, by instinct. They are not equipped, as we are, with the powers of imagination (to imagine currently unavailable options or possibilities) or the powers of assessment. Beavers, for instance, do not assess the effect that damming streams will have on the forest; they do not realize, and cannot realize, that the long-term effect is to flood the forest, deprive the root system of oxygen, and ultimately kill the trees (and eliminate the beavers' habitat!).

Humans, by contrast, do have this power of assessment, and can therefore make such assessments about long-term effects, *before* (or after) building bridges, dams, or highways. Indeed, compared to the other creatures, humans have comparatively few instincts. We are born, apparently, with a suckling instinct, a gag reflex, and a fear of heights or falling, but with few others. Our behaviors are determined by training and by reflection (whether cultural or individual). Socrates, therefore, understood human nature correctly when he observed that "the unexamined life is not worth living *for a human*."[1] Among the creatures, only humans have the capacity to examine, ponder, and compare choices. This is why Mark Twain rightly observed that the human is the only creature who *can* blush and the only one who has *reason* to.

Thus, participating in the ethical enterprise is itself a humane act. When you find yourself asking whether you should have your aging mother come live with you or whether you should put her

1. Plato, *The Apology of Socrates*, 38a. Emphasis mine, because so many translations of the *Apology* inexplicably omit this important phrase from the original Greek.

in a home with medical care, even before you answer the question, you are doing what only humans can do, because the other creatures do not raise such questions. When you wrestle with whether you will permit your daughter to train for gymnastics five afternoons a week, you are functioning as a human, even before you arrive at an answer. That is, it is ethically right to raise such ethical questions, even before you answer them. Ethics is therefore not merely about answering choice-questions correctly; it is also about *asking* them in the first place and learning to ask the kinds of questions that might yield good answers.

Ethics, as I construe it, constitutes the *disciplined reflection on human choice-making*. As such, it seeks understanding, organization, and scholarly discussion. It is responsive to (disciplined by) pertinent information from related disciplines such as philosophy, anthropology, and theology, and it is also responsive to (disciplined by) scholarly give-and-take—interactions with those whose views of some matters differ.

The Choice between Good and Better

Since I regard ethics as the disciplined reflection on choice-making, I also regard choice-making more broadly than do some. We do not ordinarily merely choose between "good" and "evil"; we just as frequently choose between "good" and "better."

It was not wrong or evil for Martha, for example, to be involved in "much serving" (Luke 10:40). In and of itself, serving others is commended throughout the Scriptures. But in this particular circumstance, Mary had made a *better* choice. By attending to Jesus's instruction, she had "*chosen* the good portion" (v. 42), so her choice was praised in comparison to the choice of Martha. One choice was good—the other was better.

Similarly, the apostle Paul wrote many letters to the churches, and yet he would have preferred to have been personally present, as he said to the Galatians: "I wish I could be present with you now and change my tone, for I am perplexed about you" (Gal. 4:20). Writing a letter was good; visiting the Galatians would have been better (see also 1 Thess. 2:17; 3:10; 3 John 1:14).

The ethical task is designed, therefore, not merely to distinguish good from evil but to distinguish good from better. Virtually by definition, an individual who habitually makes the better choice throughout life lives a better life than does another individual who habitually makes the less-good choice.

Background to the Models

Many years ago, I appreciated reading Avery Dulles's *Models of the Church*, an articulate, well-organized presentation of different functioning "models" of ecclesiology and church life. Dulles's ability to conceptualize models (or *heuristics*, or *paradigms*, as some might call them) was very helpful to me, and I suspect his influence may account for my endeavor to understand Christian ethics in terms of ethical models. I have found it helpful to think not only in terms of ethical *issues* but also in terms of ethical "models"—*ways of asking questions about life and its options*—within a Christian theistic framework. What follows is an introductory study of five models of Christian ethics, models that are derived from the Christian Scriptures and that have substantially influenced the Christian church.

During my seminary years, I found Professor John M. Frame's classes to be challenging and stimulating. His teaching on perspectivalism influenced me at a formative time, and I suspect his influence on my thinking in this area is far more comprehensive than I am consciously aware. One aspect of his perspectivalism is its ecumenical orientation—that being reared and catechized in a particular tradition within the church shapes one's perspective and that often what appear to be disagreements within the church are actually differing perspectives that each have a measure of truth and insight. Professor Frame is not a relativist; nor am I. To acknowledge the insight of a given perspective is not to affirm that every perspective is right or equally valid.[2] In what follows, I attempt to acknowledge that different aspects of the Christian tradition have made particular contributions to the entire church's ethical reasoning. Differing traditions "model" the ethical enterprise differently, and the combination of these models yields more fruit than any one would yield by itself.

In my early years of teaching at Gordon-Conwell Theological Seminary in Massachusetts, my interest in ethical models grew. There were already two ethicists on faculty: Stephen Mott and Jack Davis, each of whom had great command of the discipline. Each tended to work in the area of ethical *issues* (as do most ethicists); Jack had a special interest in medical ethics in those years, while Stephen was more interested in social and economic issues. So the seminary needed no one else to teach in the area of ethical issues, and I began working in the area of ethical hermeneutics or models. This ultimately resulted in my teaching a class on a biblical theology of ethics, during the course of which I recognized that there were five different models of ethics within the Scriptures themselves: imitation, law, wisdom, communion, and warfare.

The Five Models

The five models of ethics may be thought of as *question* clusters. Each model asks a different set of questions, and each of these sets of questions brings its own insight to the ethical program.

The law model, for instance, asks whether a potential behavioral choice is either prescribed or proscribed by God in Holy Scripture —whether the behavior is required or forbidden. By comparison, the wisdom model asks what kinds of effects and consequences that

2. It is not my concern here to enter into critical discussion of the merits/ demerits of Frame's perspectivalism. I do note, however, that he frames the matter in philosophical terms (normative, situational, and existential), which has probably left some laypeople unpersuaded (or unpersuadable?) of his views. My selection of five models that manifestly appear in Scripture may be more attractive or palatable to some. See John M. Frame, *The Doctrine of the Christian Life*, A Theology of Lordship (Phillipsburg, NJ: P&R Publishing, 2008).

potential behavioral choice is likely to have. Biblical proverbs *commend*, whereas biblical laws *command*. The wisdom literature routinely discusses the likely consequences of certain behavioral choices and thereby invites us to consider the effects of different behavioral choices. Its approach to the ethical task is therefore more contemplative, and less urgent, than that of the law model. The law model recognizes that there are moments in life when such contemplation may very well be a luxury we cannot afford to indulge. Certain behaviors, whose consequences are virtually always catastrophic, are prohibited outright.

My point throughout this work is that the five models derived from the Holy Scriptures are complementary (like a string quintet; try Schubert's in C Major) and that, therefore, we gain the fullest ethical perspective when we permit each of the models to bring its own particular cluster of questions to bear on the matter at hand.

To put it another way, each of the five models is like a different tool in the hand of a mechanic. Each of these tools, while performing a different function, works toward the same goal. The goal is a well-functioning automobile, but it cannot be achieved with only screwdrivers, or only wrenches, or only pliers. A number of tools is necessary, ordinarily, to complete a single job. Similarly, each of the ethical models that are found in the Holy Scriptures is necessary, yet insufficient in itself, to inform the ethical task.

We encounter many apparent "dead ends" in Christian discussions of ethics because we bring too few tools to the task. We ask, for instance, only law model questions, or only wisdom model questions, without asking other, equally important questions. In this book, my intent is to provide a brief, working discussion of the various major ethical models found in the Scriptures, in the hope that readers will become familiar with them, both conceptually and functionally.

The Structure of This Book

The first chapter of our study consists of an abbreviated discussion of the five models, so that each of the five may be set in comparison to the others. The following five chapters comprise more specific discussions of each of the models in turn, to demonstrate how one might employ them.

It need hardly be said that thinking rightly about life does not mean that one will live rightly. Marksmen do not always hit their target, even when it is well-defined and clear to them. Similarly, neither I nor my readers will necessarily live in a manner more consistent with God's purposes simply by thinking rightly about these matters. Indeed, moral vision is different from an ethical system; moral and ethical vision also include motivation, which tends to flow out of the understanding that evil is truly evil, destructive, and abhorrent, whereas virtue is lovely and life-giving. Refining our ability to think correctly about ethics does not assure that we will be moved to love, embrace, or pursue the ethic we thereby discover. However, it is unlikely that we will live well *without* thinking well, so we ought to make whatever efforts we can to understand the ethical enterprise better.

This short volume on ethics is not designed to enter (or settle) the more technical arena of professional or academic ethical theory. Its intention is practical and ecclesiological—to help practicing Christians to think more thoroughly Christianly about the choices we face in life. To this end, I have deliberately avoided cluttering the manuscript with footnotes that enter into those more technical discussions. I am, however, deeply grateful to the various authors in the technical study of ethics, and I have been influenced by some of them in all that follows. For the sake of my intended readership, however, I deliberately resist interacting with that scholarship in this book.

ACKNOWLEDGMENTS

This book grew out of lectures I originally gave at Gordon-Conwell Theological Seminary in the late 1980s and early 1990s in a course entitled "A Biblical Theology of Ethics," in which I attempted to trace how the Holy Scriptures addressed human behavior by following the unfolding of biblical revelation historically. In the process, I discovered what I thought were five different ways in which biblical revelation addressed human choice-making. The students in that course for several years made many helpful comments and raised many thoughtful questions (and an occasional eyebrow). Several suggested that the models would/could/should prove very helpful for laypeople, so I reworked the material, undertook to teach it orally in several churches over the years, and included much of it in the humanities courses I taught for many years at Grove City College. One former Gordon-Conwell student, Dr. A. Craig Troxel at Westminster Seminary California, has particularly ~~nagged~~ encouraged me to put the material in writing that would be accessible to laypeople and to church officers. If the publication does not please him, I trust it will at least placate him.

P&R Publishing was again a pleasure to work with (this is the third book I have published with P&R). Dave Almack was very encouraging in our early discussions, and Amanda Martin and Joy Woo made many editorial suggestions that have greatly improved the project.

1

INTRODUCTION TO THE FIVE MODELS

The Bible is a big book, and the Christian view of life is large and comprehensive. Therefore, throughout the church's history, various individuals and groups have endeavored to summarize the nature and practice of Christianity. Such summaries are intended to organize and clarify a reality that otherwise may appear too hard to grasp. What is true of Christianity in general is also true of Christian-theistic ethics. A genuinely Christian ethic is an expansive and potentially complex reality, a reality that may also need some sort of summary to provide organization.

I refer to these organizational efforts as *models*. According to the 1987 *American Heritage Dictionary and Electronic Thesaurus*, a model is "a tentative description of a system or theory that accounts for all of its known properties." I would suggest that five such descriptions of Christian ethics have endured throughout the church's history, assisting many in their efforts to live in a theistic manner. These models are the imitation model, the law model, the wisdom model, the communion model, and the warfare model.

The Imitation Model

The imitation model understands human life to consist, ideally, in our being like God on a creaturely scale. The human is understood to have been originally created in God's image, with the potential capacity to reflect many of God's praiseworthy attributes (except for what the theologians call the *incommunicable attributes* of God, such as omniscience) and many of his deeds (again, except for those that are distinctive to him as Creator or Redeemer). Compared to the law model below, the imitation model perhaps emphasizes more what one *is* than what one *does*, though the creature is also called to imitate God's works. Functionally, the imitation model requires learning about God and what is praiseworthy about him (especially as he has revealed himself in the incarnation of Jesus Christ) as a means of developing a vision for living. The imitation model asks and answers the following question: Does this decision allow me (or us) to emulate God or to cultivate human traits that reflect his image? The imitation model is reflected in many traditions historically, including the Augustinian tradition, aspects of medieval monasticism, and aspects of continental Pietism.

Among the comparative strengths of this model are the following:

- Biblical-theologically, this appears to be a model that adjusts well to the distinctions between the state of innocence and the fallen state.
- It restores doxology to ethics.
- It facilitates very well a discussion of becoming, as well as doing.

Among its relative weaknesses are the following:

- It does not contain (explicitly) the (helpful) prohibitions that are such a helpful and necessary aspect of the law model.

- Catechistically, it is probably a tad slower than the law model. To catechize by this model, one would
  - study and teach the communicable attributes of God and his imitable works;
  - study and teach why those attributes are praiseworthy, with special emphasis on their praiseworthiness as revealed in the acts of redemption;
  - study and teach why it is so important to us, as creatures and as sinners, that God has such attributes;
  - study, teach, and consider ways to be more like God and less unlike him;
  - study and teach what God's primary works are (creation, providence, redemption), in an effort to determine how we can imitate them.

The Law Model

The law model understands human life to consist, ideally, in our obeying God, who has rightful authority to order his creation as he wishes. God sustains the relation of Lawgiver and Judge to his creation, and the creature must acknowledge this relation by obeying God's commands and wishes. Therefore, the law model seeks to answer the following question: Has God, in Holy Scripture, commanded or prohibited this behavior? This model was extremely influential during the Protestant Reformation, and many of the catechisms produced by the Reformers contained an exposition of the Decalogue as a guideline for living. Roman Catholic catechisms also contain an exposition of the Decalogue, and thus promote a law model approach.

The law model understands and orders human life primarily by studying and applying biblical laws or commandments. The expositions of the Decalogue found in the Larger and Shorter Catechisms of the Westminster Assembly are good and influential examples of the law model, as are similar expositions in Luther's Small Catechism and in the Heidelberg Catechism.

Among the comparative strengths of this model are the following:

- The prohibitions contained in divinely revealed law are a great protection for a fallen race.
- A discussion of our obedience to God's laws greatly facilitates a discussion of the limits of the legislative authority of creatures and creaturely institutions. Thus, it is not at all surprising that there is such a clearly articulated statement about "Christian Liberty and Liberty of Conscience" in the Westminster Confession of Faith.
- The Decalogue can be perceived, conceptually, as an expression of the two "great" Old Testament commandments: love God and love your neighbor.
- The specificity of biblical legislation is a substantial check on subjectivism.

Among its relative weaknesses are the following:

- Fallen human nature being what it is, the law model's proponents are often perceived by outsiders as pharisaical, legalistic, self-righteous, and judgmental, and this perception has some substance to it.
- Compared to the imitation model, for instance, the law model emphasizes what one *does* more than what one *is*, which can sometimes produce a fairly un-Christlike person who has nonetheless checked off the list of dos and don'ts.
- Compared to the wisdom model, it can be attractive (and stunting) to an immature believer, whose judgment needs to mature. Such an individual may be more comfortable with having his or her behavior directed exclusively by law rather than by wisdom.
- Biblical-theologically, it imposes itself into the state of innocence (both pre-fall and in the glorified state) in a manner inconsistent with the biblical testimony.

- Similarly, its practitioners sometimes tend to eternalize covenant stipulations that are not, in their biblical form, designed to be eternal or universal.

- It can lead to somewhat heated discussions about ethical choices if it excludes other models. In such cases, all differences are perceived as matters of obedience or disobedience, rather than, for example, matters of wisdom. Those who are reared in a law-model-dominant tradition (e.g., the Pharisees in the first century, or my own Reformed tradition in the twenty-first) tend to *command* what other traditions *commend*, sometimes requiring without convincing biblical warrant such things as attending two services each Sunday, reading one's Bible daily (or at all, for that matter), practicing family "worship," and so on.

The Wisdom Model

The wisdom model understands life to consist, ideally, in making wise choices moment by moment, day by day. The human is understood to have the ability to observe, and to learn from observing, that there are choices that contribute to (or detract from) order, health, and faith. Thus, the wisdom model answers the following question: What is the likely outcome of my/our doing or not doing this? The wisdom model was perhaps more common before the invention of the printing press in Europe (after which people could learn from reading the Bible, whereas before people learned from listening and observing).

The wisdom model understands and orders life by promoting the development of wisdom—that human faculty by which we strive to make wise practical choices, moment by moment. It is, of course, the model promoted by the book of Proverbs.

Among the comparative strengths of this model are the following:

- It promotes learning from both natural and special revelation.

- It promotes the development of judgment and discretion, as well as learning by trial and error.
- It accounts for that broad area of life in which believers may *commend* certain practices to one another without feeling obligated to *command*.
- The wisdom model permits believers to recognize that differences of opinion in some areas are *not* matters of obedience or disobedience.
- This model facilitates a discussion of ethical matters with those who do not necessarily recognize the authority of God speaking in Holy Scripture and may, therefore, promote a common basis for ethical conversation with unbelievers.

Among its comparative weaknesses are the following:

- It does not contain (explicitly) the (helpful) prohibitions that are such a helpful and necessary aspect of the law model.
- It is more useful for those who are more mature, less useful for those who are less mature.

The Communion Model

The communion model understands human life to consist, ideally, in communication with God. The human is understood to have the unique ability, among creatures, of linguistic communication—of being able to address and be addressed by God. For the communion model, prayer is not something one does occasionally, in moments or seasons of special need. Life itself is prayer, a fellowship with God. Therefore, we may employ the communion model to answer the following question: How might this option enhance or inhibit my (or our) communion with God? The communion model is also well represented historically; it profoundly influenced most forms of monasticism (in many of which speaking with humans was forbidden, in order to assure that one communicated exclusively with

God) and Pietism, and it has been embraced often by Christian communions in the East.

Among the comparative strengths of this model are the following:

- It accounts for the frequency with which prayer is urged throughout the Scriptures.
- It promotes a relational understanding of life, and a vertical relation at that.
- It promotes an awareness of the reality that, beyond revealed law, there are decisions we make that either promote or disrupt communion with God.
- It may be especially valuable in an era in which quiet time for meditation and communion with God is encroached on so frequently by communications from his creatures (telephones, cell phones, email, and so on).

Among its comparative weaknesses are the following:

- It does not contain (explicitly) the (helpful) prohibitions that are such a helpful and necessary aspect of the law model.
- Its subjectivity, without the aid of the objective teaching of Scripture, could quickly engender mysticism.

The Warfare Model

The warfare model understands life as consisting of a war, in which we are enlisted as soldiers for one side. Our duties are then thought of as both defensive and offensive, as both resisting the attacks of the enemy and attacking the enemy ourselves, gaining new ground. The warfare model helps us answer the following question: In the often invisible, yet real warfare between the forces of good and evil, will this decision likely serve the forces of good or the forces of evil? Luther was especially aware of this model (undoubtedly aided by the attempts of the Roman Church to take his life), as were the

English Puritans. William Gurnall's *The Christian in Complete Armor* is a classic statement of this model.

The warfare model understands life as a conflict—ultimately a conflict between the "seed of the woman" and the "seed of the serpent" of Genesis 3. Each individual, by this model, is encouraged to recognize the need for both defensive and offensive activity. Defensively, believers are encouraged to be ready, to be watchful, and to be alert to areas of particular vulnerability; offensively, believers are encouraged to attack the Enemy, taking ground from him.

Among the comparative strengths of this model are the following:

- It cultivates an awareness of the conflict in which we find ourselves as participants.
- It arouses an appropriate sense of holy indignation that other parties are attempting to destroy and injure the saints.
- It encourages an awareness of the importance of preparation prior to conflict.

Among its comparative weaknesses are the following:

- It does not contain (explicitly) the (helpful) prohibitions that are such a helpful and necessary aspect of the law model.
- Some may abuse it to excuse their sin ("The devil made me do it").
- Some who are influenced by this model may perceive other humans as "the bad guys" and themselves as "the good guys" in the apocalyptic struggle, leading to precisely the kind of false religion that Christ warns against in the parable of the tax collector and the Pharisee.

These five ethical models would not have enjoyed enduring influence unless there were some element of truth in them. Each naturally flows from the teaching of Scripture, and a truly biblically informed life will employ each model. Since each of these models arises from the Scriptures, each is ultimately compatible with and complementary to the others. Each, however, frames questions differently, and each, therefore, brings an important contribution to the Christian attempt to evaluate and order life biblically. Each of these models, while profoundly rich in itself, is nevertheless incomplete without the others.

Their interwoven character is profound, however, and each leads us to the others. For instance, if the law model *commands* us to "get wisdom" (Prov. 4:5), we cannot fulfill the law model without employing the wisdom model. If the imitation model requires our imitation of God, we find that Christ, in his incarnate state, did nothing on his own authority, but rather that which the Father had *commanded* him (see John 8:28). The wisdom model urges the wise of heart to "receive *commandments*" (Prov. 10:8). Indeed, when one considers the threatened curse-sanctions of the Sinai covenant ("But if you will not obey . . . then all these curses shall come upon you"—Deut. 28:15), it was unwise (wisdom model) for the Israelites to be disobedient (law model). Examples such as these could be multiplied—the point is that these models are not mutually exclusive. One cannot really function within a single model without being driven to the others.

Questions for Discussion and Reflection

1. Consider the ethical models described in this chapter. Which were most familiar to you? Which, if any, were unfamiliar?
2. Based on these initial descriptions, which model do you tend to draw on most often when evaluating ethical questions or dilemmas?
3. How do each of these five models challenge common secular understandings of ethics?
4. What is the significance of each model's reliance on the others? How do they support and guide one another?

5. Complete the following sentences and discuss with a group: My family of origin emphasized the _____ model when I was growing up. My family of origin neglected the _____ model. Give examples to flesh out your discussion.

Case Study

Develop a case study to revisit throughout this book: in brief, a situation in which an ethical decision must be made. It may be drawn from your own experience, a news story, a letter to an ethicist, a work of fiction, or some other source. It may be straightforward or complex, weighty or (seemingly) inconsequential. (In addition, if you're working through this book in a public setting, make sure it's something you're willing to share.) Jot down a few notes so you'll be able to remember the details when you return to your case study at the end of the next chapter.

2

THE IMITATION MODEL

> *Does this decision allow me (or us) to emulate God or to cultivate human traits that reflect his image?*

The imitation model may be the most comprehensive of the five models of theistic ethics. Its reach extends in a remarkable range of directions, and its distinctive properties are deeply embedded in the human condition as God has created it. The imitation model raises this question: Of the available options, does one provide greater opportunity than the others to cultivate the image of God within or the garden of God without? It is not surprising that this model has been recognized throughout the church's history, nor is it surprising that many (including myself) have understood it to be the foundational biblical model. Consider just a few of the examples one could cull from some of the church's more significant leaders:

> Why art thou proud, O man? God for thee became low. Thou wouldst perhaps be ashamed to imitate a lowly man; then at least imitate the lowly God. (Augustine, *Confessions*)

Christ is our pattern, whom we must strive to imitate. It is necessary that our pattern should be exact, that so we might see our imperfections, and be humbled for them, and live by faith in our sanctification. (Richard Sibbes, *Divine Meditations*)

Fix your eye upon himself as your pattern, and study with earnest desire to follow his holy example, and be made conformable to him.—Not to imitate the works which were proper to him as God, or as Mediator; but in his holiness, which he hath proposed to his disciples for their imitation. (Richard Baxter, *A Christian Directory*)

"Christ our Example." After "Christ our Redeemer," no words can more deeply stir the Christian heart than these. Every Christian joyfully recognizes the example of Christ, as, in the admirable words of a great Scotch commentator, a body "of living legislation," as "law, embodied and pictured in a perfect humanity." In Him, in a word, we find the moral ideal historically realized, and we bow before it as sublime and yearn after it with all the assembled desires of our renewed souls. (B. B. Warfield, "Imitating the Incarnation")

Now what is this new manner of life? How is it characterized? . . . There is no consideration more basic and important than that it is life patterned after the character of God himself. "Ye shall be perfect as your heavenly Father is perfect" (Matt. 5:48). Man's definition consists in this, that he was made in the image of God. (John Murray, "The Christian Ethic")[1]

What would Jesus do? (Charles Sheldon, *In His Steps*)

---

1. John Murray, "The Christian Ethic," in *Collected Writings of John Murray* (Edinburgh: Banner of Truth Trust, 1976), 1:175.

From the earliest days of the Christian church to the present, from the most sophisticated of Christian theologians to the simplest disciple, the imitation model has captivated those who have reflected on it. Entire generations of the church have spoken the language of the imitation model to express what it means to live as a Christian. Indeed, while Thomas à Kempis's *Imitation of Christ* is not really an imitation model of ethics or devotion, the very title of the work reflects the reality that living as a Christian was *spoken* of as imitating Christ.

The Biblical Basis for the Imitation Model

The imitation model arises naturally from the twin realities that humans alone were created in the image of God and that they are commanded, throughout the history of revelation, to be like God. Four times in the two brief verses that record God's decree to create humankind, God states that humans are made like him:

> Then God said, "Let us make man in *our image*, after *our likeness*. And let them have dominion over the fish of the sea and over the birds of the heavens and over the livestock and over all the earth and over every creeping thing that creeps on the earth." So God created man *in his own image, in the image of God* he created him; male and female he created them. (Gen. 1:26–27)

Similarly, humans are frequently commanded to do or to be things that are like God, especially as he has revealed his character in Christ:

> Speak to all the congregation of the people of Israel and say to them, You shall be holy, for I the LORD your God am holy. (Lev. 19:2)

> But I say to you, Love your enemies and pray for those who persecute you, so that you may be sons of your Father who is in heaven. For he makes his sun rise on the evil and on the good, and

sends rain on the just and on the unjust. . . . You therefore must be perfect, as your heavenly Father is perfect. (Matt. 5:44–45, 48)

A new commandment I give to you, that you love one another: just as I have loved you, you also are to love one another. (John 13:34)

For those whom he foreknew he also predestined to be conformed to the image of his Son, in order that he might be the firstborn among many brothers and sisters. (Rom. 8:29)

Therefore be imitators of God, as beloved children. (Eph. 5:1)

Indeed, the apostle John envisions the human race as being like God in its perfected state in glory:

Beloved, we are God's children now, and what we will be has not yet appeared; but we know that when he appears *we shall be like him*, because we shall see him as he is. (1 John 3:2)

In light of such passages, it is easy to agree with B. B. Warfield's comment: "Of course our text [Phil. 2] is not singular in calling upon us to make Christ our example. 'Be ye imitators of me, even as I also am of Christ Jesus,' is rather the whole burden of the ethical side of Paul's teaching."[2]

The Imitation Model and Human Nature

Humans learn by imitation. It is one of the most fundamental aspects of our created nature. Even the most academic or thoughtful individual learns far more by imitation than by critical reflection.

2. B. B. Warfield, "Imitating the Incarnation," in *The Savior of the World: Sermons Preached in the Chapel of Princeton Theological Seminary* (New York: Hodder and Stoughton, 1913), 249.

Why does a young American child speak English, and a young French child speak French? Has either of them studied both languages and chosen one over the other? Of course not. Each has simply learned what is spoken in the home.

Similarly, we make hundreds, indeed thousands, of other behavioral "choices" simply by imitating what we observe around us. This occurs so frequently that we ordinarily do not even notice it. Some years ago, when we were living in Boston Children's Hospital with our first daughter, a good friend of ours visited every Wednesday evening and every Saturday, as well as on some other occasions. After little Marian died, our parents visited for the funeral service, and when our friend left the house the night of the funeral, my father walked her to her car. She later said to me, "David, you're just like your father." I asked what she meant, and she explained that when she had visited us at Boston Children's, I always walked her to her car afterward, just as my father did the night of the funeral. It wasn't until then that I realized that, growing up in Richmond, Virginia, with a Southern gentleman as a father, I had picked up the custom of walking unaccompanied women to their cars after a visit. I had been imitating my father's behavior, unconsciously and unaware, for years.

One aspect of this capacity to learn by example is the ability to discern what is praiseworthy, excellent, or noble and to imitate it. When we hear an accomplished musician such as Yo-Yo Ma play the cello, we find ourselves thinking (or even saying), "Wow, I wish I could play cello like that." Our experience is similar when we witness anyone do something with unusual competence or excellence, whether it be a cook preparing a fine meal, an author writing a great piece of literature, a mother singing a child to sleep, an athlete breaking a world record, and so on. In each case, we as humans are almost irresistibly drawn toward an appreciation of, and an emulation of, that which we perceive as excellent.

This innate capacity to learn by imitation, an unmixed blessing to the human race as originally created in the innocent state in the garden (with no one to imitate but God himself and innocent humans), has become a mixed blessing after the fall. Now it is possible to imitate either virtue *or* vice. As John the apostle warned us, "Beloved, do not imitate evil but imitate good. Whoever does good is from God; whoever does evil has not seen God" (3 John 1:11). John understood that humans are imitators, and he recognized that, under the present fallen circumstances, this capacity can be employed for good or evil, but that the capacity remains unchanged.

The capacity to imitate was one of the great gifts God gave the human race. One aspect of our being made *imago Dei* (in the image of God) is our being made *imitatio Dei* (imitator of God). Implicit in our being made "in God's image" or "in God's likeness" is our being uniquely endowed with the capacity to *behave* as God, on a creaturely scale. The capacity to imitate, therefore, is deeply woven into the fabric of our human nature.

Indeed, had we remained innocent, it is my opinion that we would never have needed the complements of some of the other models, such as the law model; imitation would have been sufficient for most of our lives.

To illustrate this, imagine a boy, eight years old, who has been promised a visit from Grandpa to take him on his first fishing excursion. Spring arrives, and Grandpa drives up one day and asks little Billy if he's ready to go fishing. Little Billy replies with an enthusiastic affirmative, and the two get in Grandpa's car and drive to the lake. When they arrive, they walk around to the back of the car, where Grandpa opens the trunk. Without a word, he reaches in and removes his fishing pole and a large tackle box. Billy peers in, sees a smaller pole and a small tackle box, and picks them up. Wordlessly, the two walk down the dock, with pole and box in hand, and sit down at the end. Grandpa opens his tackle box, baits a hook, and drops it in the water. Billy, of course, opens his small box, somewhat clumsily baits his hook, and drops it in. Not one command is given; not a single imperative is uttered. Why does little Billy do what Grandpa does? Because, for Billy, Grandpa is the epitome of love and wisdom, and he is simply delighted to do whatever Grandpa does.

This is an imperfect illustration of Adam's existence before he sinned and of our existence in the redeemed state in heaven. When our hearts are not distorted by sin, we perceive all that is lovely and admirable in God, and, with true filial affection, we are simply delighted to be like him and to do as he does.

How the Imitation Model Functions

Then God said, "Let us make man in our image, after our likeness. And let them have dominion over the fish of the sea and over the birds of the heavens and over the livestock and over all the earth and over every creeping thing that creeps on the earth." So God created man in his own image, in the image of God he created him; male and female he created them. (Gen. 1:26–27)

Note the close relation between the human as imitator and image of God and the human as creator and cultivator. The so-called "cultural mandate" or "creation mandate" is directly and deliberately related to humanity's being created in the divine image. Just as God exercises dominion by creating all things according to his pleasure, so also the human, made in God's image, will exercise dominion over this created order on God's behalf. The imitation model therefore is comprehensive in this special sense that it is fundamental to our creational calling. If the law model governs some of our specific behavioral choices (e.g., "You shall not murder" —Ex. 20:13), the imitation model governs the entirety of our created existence. It explains why the human is creative, why the human has a will to exercise dominion, why the human is delighted by making and fashioning.

Indeed, the original environment in which this God-imitator was placed had two great latent properties: the property to delight and the property to sustain life. It was, to employ biblical language, "pleasant to the sight and good for food" (Gen. 2:9). God created the world with these twin properties, and he created his image bearer to cultivate these twin properties, to develop the latent capacities for beauty and life-sustenance.

The imitation model of ethics both explains and directs human creativity, in its most comprehensive sense. It *accounts* for our desire to make (and to delight in what others make), and it *directs* this desire. It directs the desire to cultivate and make by directing us to cultivate the created order in accord with God's purposes. It also directs the task of *self*-cultivation, because it directs us to cultivate the *imago Dei* within. Thus, it informs us of our bidirectional cultivation; it teaches us to cultivate the garden without and the image of God within.

Thus, the imitation model raises the following question (among others): Of the available options, does one provide greater opportunity than the others to cultivate the image of God within or the garden of God without? Regarding the use of our leisure time, for instance, does one form of recreation contribute to the cultivation of the image of God within or the garden of God without more than another form of recreation? The imitation model, therefore, tends to encourage recreational activity that is active rather than passive. Chess, for example, is a form of recreation that, when played as intended, cultivates patience, an expanded attention span, and sequential reasoning. It thus cultivates some of the rational and intellectual properties that the human has as God's image bearer, and it is therefore a superior choice to alternatives that cultivate none of the same properties. Consequently, the imitation model brings a certain informed caution to the twenty-first century's technological preference for recreation that is largely passive.

Similarly, the imitation model encourages the cultivation of those human traits that belong exclusively to humans as bearers of God's image. Thus, both the ox and the human have the power to move (reasonably) heavy objects. Yet the human capacity to do this is not distinctively human. The human, again, can run rapidly, but so can the antelope, so swiftness is not a distinctly human trait. Other traits, however, are distinctively human; of all the creatures God made, only the human has such traits, and if the human does not cultivate these particular traits, they will remain uncultivated, since no other creature can cultivate them. Thus, there is a special mandate for the human to cultivate such distinct traits: creativity, wisdom, language, rationality, imagination, the love of beauty, gregariousness, and many more.

Indeed, one may easily suggest here that the virtue tradition of ethics—from Aristotle to Alasdair MacIntyre[3]—is grounded precisely in the *imitatio Dei*. To imitate God does not mean merely to do, on occasion, something that God would do (e.g., act justly or mercifully); it surely means to *become* like God, on a creaturely scale, by cultivating those virtues that the human alone, as *imago Dei*, can cultivate. It means to cultivate those practices and disciplines that cultivate *us*—to develop virtue internally so that our external behaviors conform to it and derive from it. Of course, such imitation would always have been merely creaturely, even in the state of innocence, and now, it is also fraught with much sin and self-love. Nonetheless, true imitation of God requires admiring his virtues and cultivating them, which is the essence of the virtue tradition of ethics.

Imitating God's Traits and Deeds

Of course, in addition to this general and comprehensive guide to the human as image bearer and maker, the imitation model also provides more specific guidance for human existence by teaching us to imitate God's traits and his deeds, his attributes and his works. Some of God's traits or attributes cannot be imitated; theologians refer to these as the *incommunicable* attributes of God. God, for instance, is immutable; we are not. God is eternal; we are not. God is infinite; we are not. Similarly, some of God's acts or deeds cannot be imitated precisely. God created out of nothing (*ex nihilo*), whereas human creativity ordinarily begins with what exists and fashions it

---

3. See Aristotle, *Nicomachean Ethics, with an English translation by H. Rackham* (New York: Harvard University Press, 1926); Alasdair MacIntyre, *After Virtue: A Study in Moral Theory* (Notre Dame, IN: Notre Dame University Press, 1984).

for a new purpose, as when an arrowhead is made out of a rock, or when a computer chip is made out of silicon (sand).

Again, God alone can redeem. Only God can atone for human sin in the God-man Jesus Christ, and we cannot precisely imitate him in this work. However, even in these incommunicable acts, there is something for us to imitate. A novelist can, at least in his imagination, "create" a previously nonexistent world, filled with animals that talk or magicians who cast spells. Similarly, while humans cannot atone for one another's sins, they can speak winsome words that direct others to the Christian gospel, and they can, by discretion and wisdom, "cover" the imperfections of others by keeping them private (a duty, by the way, required by the ninth commandment, as understood by the Westminster Larger Catechism[4]).

As a guide to human behavior, then, the imitation model provokes a disciplined, sustained, and careful discussion of God's attributes and God's works in order to gain a vision for what we are called to imitate. Broadly, God's works consist of making, sustaining, and redeeming. Therefore, humans who are creative, or who are good stewards of the resources under their supervision, are imitating God. Similarly, humans who are redemptive (at least in the broad sense), who attempt to heal wounds, recover from injuries, or reconcile enmity, are imitating a redemptive Maker. Thus, as an ethical model, the imitation model encourages considering, at each decision-making moment, whether the choices before us allow us to imitate God by making, sustaining, or redeeming. It is always right, always praiseworthy, to imitate God, and the privilege of doing so lies before us many times every day.

The imitation model, therefore, tends to afford a comprehensive, wide-angle lens for the ethical enterprise. It invites us to consider our highest calling (imitating God) at each of life's moments, and it encourages choices that contribute to this highest calling.

As an example, some readers will recall the tragic Air Florida Flight 90 accident on January 13, 1982, when a commercial jet

---

4. See Westminster Larger Catechism, questions and answers 143–45.

crashed into the Potomac River while taking off from Washington National Airport in Washington, DC. After the plane crashed, a few survivors drifted in the freezing December waters, clinging to floating debris. An onlooker, Lenny Skutnik, jumped into the icy Potomac and rescued one of the survivors at considerable risk to himself. Now, the law model would not necessarily require Mr. Skutnik to have done this, yet we all instinctively applaud the act. Why? Because he was imitating a rescuing and redeeming God. We cannot help but admire redemption; we instinctively applaud actions that rescue the needy or the helpless, especially when they endanger the rescuer. And we applaud such activity because we are God-imitators. Whether Mr. Skutnik was consciously influenced by the imitation model, or whether his action was more instinctive, the fact remains the same—this particular model commends and approves activity that imitates the deeds of a God who makes, sustains, and redeems.

God's Deeds Are Four

God has surely done more than four things, but all that he has done falls into one of four categories. God creates, judges what he created, providentially sustains, and redeems. He makes things, he maintains or preserves things, and he repairs things that are broken. Therefore, as imitators of God's deeds, we ask ourselves at each moment: Is there an opportunity here to be like our making, judging, preserving, and repairing God? Is there an opportunity to be creative? Is there an opportunity to evaluate or judge some created thing, noticing how it has been made? Is there an opportunity to be prudent in maintaining what already exists? Is there an opportunity to repair something that is broken, whether it be a child's toy or a relationship between two friends?

What is true of God's deeds is true also of his attributes. The imitation model encourages us to reflect on the communicable attributes of God, to understand why they are praiseworthy and how we can imitate them. It encourages us to ask the following questions about each of God's traits:

21

1. What is the trait (e.g., love, wisdom, power, holiness, justice, benevolence, faithfulness, truthfulness, mercy, patience, kindness, gentleness, wrath, jealousy)?
2. What Scriptures teach that God has this trait?
3. Why is this trait praiseworthy?
4. Why is it important to us, as creatures, that God has this trait?
5. Why is it important to us, as *fallen* creatures, that God has this trait?
6. What can we do, with the aid of God's Spirit, to cultivate this trait ourselves?
7. What attitudes, affections, or behaviors prohibit the cultivation of this trait?

Whereas ancient Greek ethics often taught that virtues, such as justice, existed independently of any moral agents, in the realm of abstract ideas, the Scriptures teach that all ideal virtue is always embodied in a moral agent, and supremely so in God himself. Thus, we can inquire regarding each of these attributes—not merely abstractly, but concretely—in the character of God. By raising the questions listed above, we reflect on such virtue as it is revealed in God's character and actions, and we are drawn into both an understanding and an admiration of the trait, which leads us to emulate it. Indeed, we might even say that this model combines doxology with ethics, because it enables us to admire and adore the attributes of God, as the first step toward imitating such attributes ourselves. To examine how the imitation model works, let us take, as an example, justice.

1. What is justice?

The American Heritage Dictionary of the English Language defines justice as "the attainment of what is just, especially that which is fair, moral, right, merited, or in accordance with law." Ordinarily, Christian theologians have identified several dimensions of this trait:

- Such perfection of moral character that abhors wickedness and loves uprightness.
- The idea of moral desert.
- The notion of equity or impartiality—that people are treated without regard for their persons but with regard for what they have actually done.

2. What Scriptures teach that God has this trait?

Many Scripture passages teach God's justice. A few examples will suffice.

- *Perfection of moral character*: "For the LORD is righteous; he loves righteous deeds; the upright shall behold his face" (Ps. 11:7; see also Ps. 1:5–6).
- *Moral desert*: "He will render to each one according to his works: to those who by patience in well-doing seek for glory and honor and immortality, he will give eternal life; but for those who are self-seeking and do not obey the truth, but obey unrighteousness, there will be wrath and fury" (Rom. 2:6–8; see also Ex. 34:6–7; Pss. 58:11; 94:2; Heb. 11:6).
- *Equity or impartiality*: "If you call on him as Father who judges impartially according to each one's deeds, conduct yourselves with fear throughout the time of your exile" (1 Peter 1:17; see also Gen. 18:23–25; Ps. 96:10; Rom. 2:9–11).

3. Why is this trait praiseworthy?

First, we should candidly acknowledge that, for many, this trait is not immediately attractive. God's justice is something we as sinners may understandably fear. With our first parents, we run from God, attempting to hide from his judgment. Were it not for the principle of substitution, we could not, as sinners, heartily praise God's justice.

The principle of substitution, however, is the principle that permits God to be "just and the justifier of the one who has faith in Jesus" (Rom. 3:26). Indeed, the entire Christian doctrine of justification depends on the fact that God does indeed reward the righteous. God the Father does reward and exalt Christ for his obedience; he does give him the deserts and merits of what he has accomplished. Standing in our stead before God as a public representative, Christ achieves a righteousness that *merits* the approval of God. As A. W. Tozer put it, "Through the work of Christ in atonement, justice is not violated but satisfied when God spares a sinner. Redemptive theology teaches that mercy does not become effective toward a man until justice has done its work. The just penalty for sin was exacted when Christ our Substitute died for us on the cross."[5] Or, as it is expressed in the Westminster Confession of Faith,

> The Lord Jesus, by his perfect obedience, and sacrifice of himself, which he, through the eternal Spirit, once offered up unto God, hath fully satisfied the justice of his Father; and purchased, not only reconciliation, but an everlasting inheritance in the kingdom of heaven, for all those whom the Father hath given unto him. (8.5)

This truth is well captured by John Newton's words:

> Let us wonder;
> grace and justice join and point to mercy's store;
> when through grace in Christ our trust is,
> justice smiles, and asks no more.[6]

Second, God's justice is perhaps best appreciated when we witness its absence. When we (or others) are judged unjustly by a human judge (whether civil, ecclesiastical, or domestic), we appreciate justice by abhorring injustice. When the wicked are not held accountable for their crimes, we instinctively sense that a great wrong has been done.

5. A. W. Tozer, *The Knowledge of the Holy* (New York: Harper & Row, 1961), 88.
6. John Newton, "Let Us Love and Sing and Wonder," 1774.

When judges are bribed, we instinctively recoil. When the wealthy and powerful are shielded from accountability for their behavior before the law, we instinctively recognize the corruption of justice. When the "teacher's pet" or the "Mama's boy" is not held to the same standards as others, we instinctively object.

4. Why is it important to us, as creatures, that God has this trait?

God assures us that he is not blind to the injustice that we so commonly experience in the present fallen state. He is not unaware of the exploitation of the weak and powerless by the strong and powerful; nor is he heedless of the suffering of those who are treated unjustly. At the return of Christ, there will be an accounting for every thought, word, and deed, and the unjust will receive from the hand of God the punishment that their wickedness deserves.

5. Why is it important to us, as *fallen* creatures, that God has this trait?

As fallen creatures, we may initially fear God's justice and worry about the reality that he will "by no means clear the guilty" (Ex. 34:7; Num. 14:18; Nah: 1:3). As we consider the work of Christ, however, we understand how fully he has satisfied divine justice, and how perfect his own obedience was, which is now imputed to his people. If God truly loves and rewards the obedient and upright, and if Christ truly was obedient and upright, then he will surely be rewarded, and we are that reward. As Paul put it, "by the one man's obedience the many will be made righteous" (Rom. 5:19).

6. What can we do, with the aid of God's Spirit, to cultivate this trait ourselves?

We can ask ourselves whether we hold an office or a position where we have opportunities to be either just or unjust. Parents, for instance, ought to treat their children impartially, punishing or rewarding behaviors without partiality. Supervisors ought to review those who work for them impartially, accurately noting both strengths and weaknesses. Teachers and professors ought to grade their students impartially.

7. What attitudes, affections, or behaviors prohibit the cultivation of this trait?

False sympathy. Sympathy is appropriate when people have experienced pain or heartache; it is entirely inappropriate when we are evaluating whether someone has done right or wrong. Whenever we are called to render a judgment (whether at home, at work, or in civil or ecclesiastical court), it is entirely inappropriate to raise questions such as "Well, what will happen to him if we render this judgment?" or "How will she feel if we come to this conclusion?"

Fearing men more than God. When we are more concerned with pleasing people than pleasing God, we inevitably pervert justice by basing our decision on whether the person in question (or the person's friends, relatives, and so on) will like what we've done or not.

Partiality. We cannot permit our judgments to be influenced by personal considerations. Friend or foe, we are to evaluate, when called to do so, by consistent, impartial standards.

This exercise could be multiplied many times by examining traits such as faithfulness, goodness, kindness, jealousy, love, mercy, patience, forbearance, truth, wisdom, self-denial, and so on. In each case, we attempt to obey commands such as these:

I have given you an example, that you also should do just as I have done to you. (John 13:15)

A new commandment I give to you, that you love one another: just as I have loved you, you also are to love one another. (John 13:34)

Therefore be imitators of God, as beloved children. (Eph. 5:1)

And indeed, in the church, we undertake to show forth our imitation of God, so that others can imitate him by imitating us:

Be imitators of me, as I am of Christ. (1 Cor. 11:1)

Brothers and sisters, join in imitating me, and keep your eyes on those who walk according to the example you have in us. (Phil. 3:17)

For you yourselves know how you ought to imitate us, because we were not idle when we were with you. (2 Thess. 3:7)

Remember your leaders, those who spoke to you the word of God. Consider the outcome of their way of life, and imitate their faith. (Heb. 13:7)

So I exhort the elders among you, as a fellow elder and a witness of the sufferings of Christ, as well as a partaker in the glory that is going to be revealed: shepherd the flock of God that is among you, exercising oversight, not under compulsion, but willingly, as God would have you; not for shameful gain, but eagerly; not domineering over those in your charge, but being examples to the flock. (1 Peter 5:1–3)

When we study carefully the various attributes of God, we are preparing ourselves for the specific ethical activity of imitating God. Theology proper (the study of God) thus aids the study of ethics, by shaping our appreciation of God's attributes and thereby directing us as his imitators.

Special Challenges to the Imitation Model

The imitation model is not fast; compared to the law model's terse imperatives, it requires a substantial amount of study. Only when we know about God's traits and works can we begin to emulate them. However, even a new student of biblical truth has some knowledge of God's traits and deeds and can seek opportunities to imitate him on a creaturely scale. For instance, Jesus said, "A new commandment I give to you, that you love one another: just as I have loved you, you also are to love one another" (John 13:34). Surely this text calls attention to sacrificial love, such as that which Christ exhibited by dying on the cross.

Another challenge of the imitation model is that not all of God's traits can be imitated by a mere creature. Theologians distinguish the "communicable" attributes of God from the "incommunicable" attributes of God. The "incommunicable" attributes, such as eternity, omniscience, and omnipotence, are attributes that God alone has and that he does not share with his creatures.

Questions for Discussion and Reflection

1. How does a secular understanding of ethics prohibit the use of the imitation model? In what ways does the secular world still "borrow capital," so to speak, from the imitation model?

2. Why do we need an intimate and growing knowledge of, and relationship with, God to employ the imitation model? How can you foster this knowledge of God in your life?

3. How does our fallen nature affect our ability to employ the imitation model? List several challenges that our fallenness presents to the exercise of this model.

4. How might the imitation model fall short if we use it in isolation from the other four models?

5. Consider a situation in your own life where the imitation model could help you work through ethical questions. Describe the situation below and discuss how the imitation model provides valuable discernment.

Case Study

Return to your case study from the opening chapter and answer the following questions with it in mind.

1. What is helpful about viewing the situation through an imitation lens?
2. What aspects of the situation, if any, does the imitation model not seem to address?
3. Based on the imitation model, what decision(s) would you advise a person in this situation to make? Why?
4. Are you satisfied with how the imitation model addresses this situation? Why or why not?

3

THE LAW MODEL

> *Has God, in Holy Scripture, commanded or prohibited this behavior?*

As we have seen, the law model understands life to consist, in part, in the relation of the Creator to his creatures, of the Lawgiver to his subjects. God has the rightful authority to direct and rule that which he has made. Thus, he may command the lesser light to rule the night and the greater light to rule the day (see Gen. 1:16). He assigns roles, functions, and responsibilities to his creatures, and he often does so in the form of commands, imperatives, or laws. As a model of ethics, then, the law model asks, Has God commanded anything relevant to the matter at hand? Has he prescribed or proscribed anything?

The law model of ethics acknowledges two essential realities. First, it acknowledges God's *right* to govern us:

> Know that the LORD, he is God!
> > It is he who made us, and we are his;
> > we are his people, and the sheep of his pasture. (Ps. 100:3)

You were bought with a price. So glorify God in your body.
(1 Cor. 6:20)

We are *created* by God ("It is he who made us"), we are providentially
sustained by him ("the sheep of his pasture"), and we are *redeemed*
by him ("bought with a price"), so we are thrice obligated to serve
him. Second, the law model acknowledges the *wisdom* and *love* by
which God governs us well:

As a father shows compassion to his children,
     so the LORD shows compassion to those who fear him.
For he knows our frame;
     he remembers that we are dust. (Ps. 103:13–14)

Thus, God's creating us not only grants him the *authority* to rule us,
but it also ensures that he *knows* us well and is therefore *qualified*,
by love and wisdom, to rule for our benefit.

Biblical Basis for the Law Model

The law model is derived from the persistence of divinely
revealed commands in the Bible. In the original account of creation,
for instance, God not only creates but also, in the very act, issues a
decree for how each aspect of what he has created is to serve him.
Effectively, he *commands* each aspect of the created order to serve
him by fulfilling a particular task, including the human's task to
"have dominion over the fish of the sea and over the birds of the
heavens and over the livestock and over all the earth and over every
creeping thing that creeps on the earth" (Gen. 1:26). And indeed,
all human suffering results from Adam's *disobedience* of God's pro-
hibition against eating the fruit of one particular tree (see Gen.
2:16–17; 3:6, 17; Rom. 5:19). Later, the covenant administration
inaugurated at Mount Sinai through Moses is surely characterized
by laws; at the institution of the covenant itself, Moses brings down

"ten words"[1] from the mountain, at least nine of which are commands (some traditions believe that all ten are commands). Much later, when the resurrected Christ is about to ascend to heaven, he instructs his apostles to teach others "to observe all that I have *commanded* you" (Matt. 28:20).

The Law Model and Human Nature

The law model has played a dominant, perhaps even predominant, role in the church's discussion of ethics, especially since the Protestant Reformation. Luther's Small Catechism (1529) contains an exposition of the Decalogue, as do the Heidelberg Catechism (1563) and both the Shorter and Larger Catechisms of the Westminster Assembly (1647). The Protestant tradition has found it catechistically helpful to summarize Christian duty by employing the ten words given at Sinai, though the law model does not restrict itself to the ten words. Indeed, the law model could function just as well by employing the two great commands (see Lev. 19:18; Deut. 6:4–5), the "new commandment" (John 13:34), or some other summary of the law (such as 1 Cor. 13 or Phil. 2). The particular structure of the law model is less significant than the fact that it recognizes God's rightful *authority* to rule us, as well as his wisdom and love that make his rule a *blessing* to us. Wherever these twin realities are prominent in the ethical enterprise, the law model is alive and well.

The benefits of the law model are substantial. It promotes appropriate creaturely humility, as we recognize that we exist under the

---

1. The original Hebrew does not contain the expression "ten commandments," nor does the Greek Bible. In Exodus 34:28 and Deuteronomy 4:13; 10:4, the Hebrew refers to ten *debarim* ("words"). The expression "ten commandments" appears in some English translations, nearly all of which have a marginal note indicating that the Hebrew says "ten words." Many English translations follow the Hebrew Old Testament, the Greek Old Testament, the Latin Vulgate, and Luther's *Die Bibel* by translating "ten words," e.g., Common English Bible, Complete Jewish Bible, Darby, Douay-Rheims American Edition, Lexham English Bible, The Message, New American Bible (Revised Edition).

authority of our Maker. It provides profoundly rich and specific directives for many human questions (e.g., "You shall not murder," "You shall not commit adultery," "You shall not steal," "You shall not covet"—Ex. 20:13–15, 17; Rom. 13:9). The human race is not left alone to discover every ethical answer by trial and error. God, as the Governor of the human race, has issued some specific commands that direct us in healthy paths and protect us from unhealthy ones. His laws are analogous to a parent's stern and forceful command to a young child: "Don't touch that stove!"

Indeed, the law model is especially necessary for us in our fallen condition, because our affections and desires have been perverted by sin. Like the child who reaches up to touch a hot stove, we exhibit an unhealthy curiosity to explore dangerous areas, and many of God's laws are framed negatively, to prohibit those behaviors that are most likely to harm us (or others) and degrade God's image within us. The apostle Paul appears to have been acutely aware that sinners need laws, because he always locates "law" in the post-fallen state:

> Sin indeed was in the world before the law was given. (Rom. 5:13)

> Why then the law? It was added because of transgressions. (Gal. 3:19)

Indeed, Paul goes so far as to say,

> Now we know that the law is good, if one uses it lawfully, under-standing this, that the law is not laid down for the just but for the lawless and disobedient, for the ungodly and sinners, for the unholy and profane, for those who strike their fathers and mothers, for murderers, the sexually immoral, men who practice homosexuality, enslavers, liars, perjurers, and whatever else is contrary to sound doctrine. (1 Tim. 1:8–10)

Some commentators think that Paul is speaking hyperbolically here, because of some special circumstances at Ephesus, but there is every reason to take his statement at face value, as a candid recognition of the need for law to govern sinful people. However we resolve the interpretive question, and whatever we might speculate regarding the utility of law even for the innocent, biblical commands are certainly a special and necessary aid for us in our yet-fallen condition. They are a kind gift from God for those whose moral nature is fallen, just as a parent's warning about the hot stove is an act of kindness.

How the Law Model Functions

The law model functions in a fairly straightforward way. As we consider any behavioral choice, the law model asks whether God commands or prohibits the behavior in question. If we find ourselves wondering whether it is right to desire another person's possessions, we find that God's law prohibits covetousness (Ex. 20:17; Rom. 13:9). If we find ourselves in a malicious rage, desiring to injure someone, we find that his law prohibits both murder (Ex. 20:13) and malicious thoughts (Matt. 5:22). If we wonder what our duty is to our parents, we discover that God commands us to honor them (Ex. 20:12; Eph. 6:2). Indeed, perhaps it is this specificity that makes the law model such an efficient model for ethics, and it may be why the law model has predominated in so many circles. Alas, however, appearances can be deceiving. There are a number of special challenges inherent in the law model, challenges that make the model less immediately efficient than it first appears.

Special Challenges to the Law Model

The special challenges inherent in the law model are due to the fact that, while the equivalent of an imperative mood in Hebrew or Greek is fairly easy to discern, some commands recorded in Scripture do not oblige everyone. We must learn to distinguish commands that oblige us from commands that do not oblige us.[2] Specifically, we must distinguish three things: local or particular laws from general or universal laws, temporary laws from eternal laws, and specific covenant stipulations from general moral principles. Each of these is a unique challenge, so we must consider briefly how to make such distinctions.

Local or Particular Laws versus General or Universal Laws

Some commands in Scripture are addressed to specific individuals or groups, and they do not oblige us to the duty contained in them; they only oblige us to believe that God gave that duty to particular individuals or groups. For example, Paul gives this command to Timothy: "When you come, bring the cloak that I left with Carpus at Troas, also the books, and above all the parchments" (2 Tim. 4:13). Evidently, this is a particular command that obliges only Timothy, and common sense probably prevents anyone from misapplying the command as a universal imperative. However, several verses earlier (4:5), Paul commanded, "As for you, always be sober-minded, endure suffering, *do the work of an evangelist*, fulfill your ministry." The italicized part of this exhortation is regularly understood to be universal or general, despite the fact that the immediately following words ("fulfill *your* ministry") suggest that the command is specific to Timothy.

While there are probably no interpretive rules that will resolve every questioned application of a local or particular command, there are strategies that can help in many, if not most, circumstances. Perhaps the most effective strategy is to ask a simple twofold question: To whom was the command originally given? Is my relation to God (or to someone else issuing the command, such as Paul) the same as that of the individual or group to whom the command was given?

---

2. In what follows, I can provide only the briefest introduction to this complex topic. An entire volume could easily be devoted to the issues associated with biblical law, and indeed such volumes have been written, e.g., Patrick Fairbairn, *The Revelation of Law in Scripture* (Edinburgh: T. & T. Clark, 1869); Vern S. Poythress, *The Shadow of Christ in the Law of Moses* (Brentwood, TN: Wolgemuth & Hyatt, 1991).

Thus, in the example above, Timothy was an ordained minister and a fellow worker with Paul who, especially when Paul was imprisoned, routinely ran particular errands for him, taking letters and financial collections to and from various churches. Not all of us are Paul's coworkers, and not all of us are ordained ministers.

As another example, we do not require, for church membership, that individuals sell all that they have and give it to the poor (see Luke 18:22). Jesus required this of the rich young ruler because, in his particular case, his dependence on earthly wealth was a barrier to his spiritual health. The command, therefore, was local and particular —it was incumbent on him but not necessarily on any or all others.

Temporary Laws versus Eternal Laws

Similarly, some laws in Scripture are temporary obligations rather than obligations for all people for all time. Many of the Mosaic laws obliged the old covenant Israelites but do not oblige new covenant believers (e.g., circumcision, the ceremonial laws, the civil laws). What makes this difficult is that some of these laws *did* oblige God's visible covenant people for hundreds of years, and it was very hard for the first generation of the Christian covenant to abandon them. The Jerusalem Council recorded in Acts 15 candidly reveals that the apostles themselves did not have an immediate answer to the problem, and Paul's issues with the Galatians (and Peter!) indicate that the problem did not resolve itself easily or immediately (see Gal. 2:11–14).

What makes some of these commands especially difficult is the fact that they are often described, in English translations, as being "eternal," "forever," or "everlasting." The rite of circumcision is abolished in the new covenant and replaced by the rite of baptism. Yet, when he originally instituted the rite, God said to Abraham, "Both he who is born in your house and he who is bought with your money, shall surely be circumcised. So shall my covenant be in your flesh an everlasting covenant" (Gen. 17:13). Similarly, when the Lord instituted the Day of Atonement for the Israelites, as part of their regular calendar, he said that "it is a statute forever" (Lev. 16:31). The Feast of Firstfruits is called "a statute forever throughout your generations" (Lev. 23:14), even though the entire Jewish calendar expired with the resurrection of Christ. These, and many other Old Testament laws and ordinances, are described in a manner that suggests that they are everlasting, even though the subsequent teaching of the New Testament makes it clear that they are not.

Part of this is a translation difficulty. The Hebrew idiom that can mean "forever" in some circumstances can also mean "for an age" or "for a long time." In contexts in which covenants and their stipulations are being described, it might even be accurately translated "in perpetuity" or "until I say otherwise." The point is that these stipulations are not restricted to twenty or thirty years, such as our home mortgage contracts; they are put in place until God changes the covenant itself. John Owen rightly recognized this reality when he said, "The 'for ever' of the old testament was the duration of the dispensation of the old covenant."[3]

The task of distinguishing temporary from everlasting commands, therefore, is not as simple as it first appears. We must be willing to distinguish commands that delineate the relation between creatures and their Creator from those that merely last for the duration of a given covenant administration. Indeed, it is to this third distinction that we now turn.

Specific Covenant Stipulations versus General Moral Principles

In a technical sense, the Bible contains no universal laws as we, influenced by Greek philosophy, understand them. All of the biblical laws are in fact covenant stipulations, and they are placed by God on the party or parties with whom he covenants. When he "commands" the stormy winds to fulfill his word (Ps. 148:8), or when he assigns a limit to the sea, that it may not transgress his command (see Prov. 8:29), humans are under no obligation to keep these commands. When God made a particular covenant with the Israelites and gave

---

3. John Owen, *The Works of John Owen* (Edinburgh: Banner of Truth, 1968), 11:490.

her laws—some of which required that she remain separate from the other nations—he did not intend, in that revelatory act itself, to say anything to those nations around her.

This is why Paul could say that the one distinctive privilege of the Israelites was that they "were entrusted with the oracles of God" (Rom. 3:2). Although some of these stipulations bear a moral obligation that extends beyond the particular covenant in which they were first recorded, *as* originally given, they oblige only those to whom God gave them. Just as I am not obligated to make mortgage payments to your banker, nor you to my banker, because we are contracted only to our own respective bankers, so also the commands in the Bible always appear in a given covenantal context—they are addressed to (and therefore oblige only) a specific covenant people.

Indeed, this is true even of the Decalogue. Though it has been helpfully employed as a catechetical tool by the church, technically speaking, the ten words are also covenant stipulations, addressed to those whom God delivered from the Egyptians. As Stuart Robinson put it,

> You are now ready to ask—What then is the nature and purpose of the Sinai revelations: and what place and relation do they hold in the gospel system? The answer to this question is not left to our conjecture or to mere ingenious inference. In much fuller detail than in the case of any of the preceding revelations is the whole matter expounded for us by the scriptures themselves. This is a *covenant transaction*, and this law, so called, constitutes simply *the stipulations of that covenant*. So it is expressly declared of it, "The Lord our God made a *covenant* with us at Horeb." It was ratified formally, as a *covenant*, when first received, the people being called upon solemnly to swear it, after it had been written down in a book.[4]

---

4. Stuart Robinson, *Discourses of Redemption* (Richmond: Presbyterian Committee of Publication, 1866), 124. Emphases mine.

Since the various commands of the Bible are always delivered in a given covenantal context, how do we determine that some of these commands oblige others also? The following seven guidelines may help.

1. Is a given law (or body of laws) reiterated in another covenant administration? This does not, of itself, prove that the law in question is pan-covenantal (e.g., circumcision is required within both the Abrahamic and the Sinai covenants, but not in the new covenant). However, such evidence does indicate at least that the given law is not restricted to a single covenant.

2. Is a given law (or body of laws) reiterated in the covenant in which we find ourselves? This alone would settle the issue for us, in terms of *our* duty. So, when Paul reiterates certain Old Testament commands in places such as Romans 13 and Ephesians 5, we are at least sure that those commands oblige members of the new covenant community.

3. Is a given law (or body of laws) supplied prior to the fall? Excepting the specific probationary law ("Of the tree of the knowledge of good and evil you shall not eat"—Gen. 2:17), such laws would probably reveal the will of God for the creature per se.

4. Does a given command describe the final, redeemed state? If so, and apart from any necessary constraints in the history of redemption, such revelation would be free of covenantal restrictions and would refer to ideal, restored human existence in the final state of innocence.

5. Is a given law supplied with a rationale that is extra-covenantal? Even though a given command may originally appear as a stipulation of a particular covenant, it is possible that the rationale supplied with the command is permanent, in which case the command itself is permanent. This was the reasoning of Charles Hodge, who said, "If the reason or ground for a given law is permanent, the law itself is permanent."[5]

Sabbatarians, for example, have rightly argued that some kind of Sabbath observance is obligatory even beyond the Sinai covenant, because the command itself, as recorded in Exodus, is grounded in the *general* realities of creation and consummation, realities that bracket all of human existence (see Ex. 20:8–11). It should be noted, however, that the form of the command as recorded in Deuteronomy 5 is grounded in the *particular* reality of God's having delivered the Israelites from slavery in Egypt (see Deut. 5:12–15). Within the Sinai administration itself, then, the same command has both a general and a particular rationale. Some of the ongoing questions among Sabbatarians (e.g., so-called "blue laws") may reflect the reality that certain aspects of Israel's Sabbath observance were unique to her, while other aspects were common to the human race, which was created to move toward its consummation Sabbath in the age to come, when the saints will "rest from their labors" (Rev. 14:13).

6. Does a given command reflect a moral attribute of God, whom we were created to imitate? For example, Moses recorded these words:

> He executes justice for the fatherless and the widow, and loves the sojourner, giving him food and clothing. Love the sojourner, therefore, for you were sojourners in the land of Egypt. (Deut. 10:18–19)

The command to love the fatherless, the widow, and the sojourner is grounded in the reality that God, in whose image we are created, loves them. All such commands obligate all humans, because all humans are created to imitate God.

---

5. Charles Hodge, *Systematic Theology* (Grand Rapids: Eerdmans, 1978), 3:268.

7. Does the content of a given command reflect the distinctive features of a given covenant administration? The vast majority of biblical imperatives are revealed within the Sinai covenant administration. Therefore, it is helpful to note what the distinctive features of this administration are, in order to discern when the stipulations of that covenant reflect universal realities and when they reflect distinctive, or particular, realities. Three distinctive realities of the Sinai covenant administration help us to evaluate how her stipulations relate to other covenants.

First, Israel was a peculiar ethnic and covenantal people. God chose the seed of Abraham and made special promises to Abraham and his seed: to make them a nation, to give them a land, and to bless all the nations of the earth through Abraham's seed (see Gen. 12:1–3; 15; 22:15–18). Because God purposed to bless the nations in this way, he required that the Israelites remain separate from other ethnic peoples as a means of preserving the Abrahamic lineage. As Moses reminded them, "For you are a people holy to the LORD your God. The LORD your God has chosen you to be a people for his treasured possession, out of all the peoples who are on the face of the earth" (Deut. 7:6; see also 14:2; Ex. 19:6).

For this reason, we should expect that many of Israel's covenant stipulations would require the Israelites to distinguish themselves in a variety of ways from the nations around them. And, indeed, this is what we find. Circumcision, the Jewish calendar, and the dietary code all are designed to distinguish Israel from the surrounding nations and to remind her that she is a particular covenant people. Later, when the gentiles *also* come to believe in Abraham's God through the death and resurrection of Christ (whom Paul identifies as the "offspring" of Abraham in Gal. 3:16), we are not at all surprised to find that the laws that distinguished Israel from other peoples are abolished, as Paul argues in Galatians.

Second, Israel was a theocracy, a geopolitical entity in which God was King. God played the role of a king when he delivered the Israelites from Egypt, and when he provided for them in the wilderness with manna from heaven, quail, and water from a rock. Similarly, he played the role of a king when he delivered a covenant to them that constituted them as a particular nation at Sinai. As a sovereign, he imposed his covenant treaty on them, royally enacting the terms by which he would interact with them. He also functioned as a king during the conquest of the land, when the Israelites, with no formal military or monarchy, were led by a succession of divinely appointed and divinely equipped judges who, armed with the Spirit of God (and sometimes with little else), conquered the indigenous peoples of the land, often committing *cherem* warfare, by which the indigenous peoples, and all their possessions, were completely eradicated. And indeed, when the Israelites insisted that Samuel appoint a monarch for them, so that they could be like the other nations, God perceived this as a rejection of his kingship (see 1 Sam. 8). Their desire to have a mixed, or blended, theocracy, in which Yahweh ruled alongside a visible, standing monarchy and military, was an implicit rejection of God's theocratic design for Israel.

Nonetheless, God's laws and covenant did not change, and his laws remained theocratic. The laws of Moses still required Israel to be a "holy" people, dwelling in a "holy" land (see Lev. 19:2; Ps. 78:54). All the inhabitants of this land, within this holy theocracy, were obliged to obey the laws of the land and were protected by the same laws, even the stranger within the gates (see Ex. 20:10; Deut. 5:14). And, because the entire society was to embody the reign of God, blasphemers faced capital punishment (see Lev. 24:16).

Yet when Jesus arrived on earth, he expressly stated that his kingdom was non-theocratic. His kingdom was "not of this world" (John 18:36), and he urged his followers to render to God what was God's and to Caesar what was Caesar's (see Matt. 22:21; Mark 12:17; Luke 20:25), an impossible distinction within a theocratic society. Therefore, in this second area also, we would expect that those covenant stipulations related to the Israelite theocracy would surely not continue into the new covenant, since the new covenant is non-theocratic.

We see an example of this in 1 Corinthians 5, where "a man has his father's wife" (5:1). In the Israelite theocracy, such an act was a capital crime: "If a man lies with his father's wife, he has uncovered his father's nakedness; both of them shall surely be put to death; their blood is upon them" (Lev. 20:11). But Paul does *not* require the death penalty for either party—rather, he requires that the man be excommunicated (5:5). Further, there is implicit evidence that this individual is eventually restored to the church (2 Cor. 2:5–11), an impossibility under the theocratic law that would have executed him. In the theocracy, the covenant people had the authority and the responsibility to execute certain categories of offenders; in the non-theocracy, the covenant people do not have this authority. And indeed, Paul does not appear to teach that the civil magistrate ought to execute such people either—rather, it ought to punish evildoers in a general, moral sense, not in a theocratic or religious sense (see Rom. 13).[6]

Third, the Sinai covenant administration included blessings and cursings of a temporal and conditional nature. When the Israelites committed themselves to the covenant, six tribes were required to shout from Mount Gerizim the blessings of the covenant, and six tribes were required to shout from Mount Ebal the cursings of the covenant (see Deut. 27). As Moses summarized the nature of this covenant, with its blessings and cursings, note the symmetry:

And if you faithfully obey the voice of the LORD your God, being careful to do all his commandments that I command you today, . . . all these blessings shall come upon you and overtake you, if you obey the voice of the LORD your God.	But if you will not obey the voice of the LORD your God or be careful to do all his commandments and his statutes that I command you today, then all these curses shall come upon you and overtake you.

6. For a fuller discussion, see T. David Gordon, "Critique of Theonomy: A Taxonomy," *Westminster Theological Journal* 56 (Spring 1994): 23–43.

Blessed shall you be in the city, and blessed shall you be in the field. Blessed shall be the fruit of your womb and the fruit of your ground and the fruit of your cattle, the increase of your herds and the young of your flock. Blessed shall be your basket and your kneading bowl. Blessed shall you be when you come in, and blessed shall you be when you go out. (Deut. 28:1–6)

Cursed shall you be in the city, and cursed shall you be in the field. Cursed shall be your basket and your kneading bowl. Cursed shall be the fruit of your womb and the fruit of your ground, the increase of your herds and the young of your flock. Cursed shall you be when you come in, and cursed shall you be when you go out. (Deut. 28:15–19)

We may observe three things about this blessing and cursing. First, we note the general symmetry of the two: blessing is not greater than cursing, nor is cursing greater than blessing. Second, we note that the blessings and cursings are conditional: if Israel is obedient, Yahweh will bless her; if she is disobedient, Yahweh will curse her. Third, we note that the blessings and cursings are temporal, not eternal; they are material, not spiritual. Neither heaven itself, nor any of its eschatological blessings, are promised to Israel on the condition of her obedience. All that God pledges is temporal prosperity in the earthly land of Canaan.

These conditional and temporal blessings and cursings are a distinctive feature of the Sinai covenant administration. In the Abrahamic covenant, the promised blessings were *not* contingent on Abraham's obedience. God simply promised to old Abraham and barren Sarah that he would grant them descendants (see Gen. 17:15–21). There was nothing this elderly couple could do, nothing in their natural ability, to produce children; they were well beyond the childbearing years. Yet God gave them Isaac as a gift—and, of course, as part of his ultimate plan to bless the nations through Abraham's seed.

Even the stipulation of this covenant did not make it conditional in the Sinai sense. God required Abraham to be circumcised and to circumcise all of the males in his house, both those bought with money and those born therein (see Gen. 17:9–14). Yet how could Abraham have circumcised Isaac, unless God had already kept his gracious promise to *give* him a descendant? Abraham could not have circumcised those born in his house, unless, by special divine blessing, he had someone to circumcise. The fulfilled promise, we might say, preceded the stipulation.

Circumcision, therefore, was not a *condition* of the blessing. At Sinai, by contrast, the conditions must be fulfilled *before* the temporal blessings come (and this is why the original generation of Moses never entered the promised land of Canaan—they were disobedient [see Num. 14:28–30]). Abraham did some unwise and unfaithful things, such as attempting to procure a descendant through Hagar (see Gen. 16) and prevaricating about whether Sarah was his wife or his sister (see Gen. 12:10–20), yet he received the blessing of a son. Moses's generation did some unwise and unfaithful things, such as murmuring against Moses and Aaron and complaining about God's provision of manna and quail (see Num. 14 and 21), and they did *not* receive the blessing of inheriting the land of Canaan.

Paul contrasts the two covenants in Galatians 3, precisely on the point that, at Sinai, a conditional curse enters the covenantal scene:

> And the Scripture, foreseeing that God would justify the Gentiles by faith, preached the gospel beforehand to Abraham, saying, "In you shall all the nations be *blessed*." So then, those who are of faith are *blessed* along with Abraham, the man of faith.
>
> For all who rely on works of the law are under a *curse*; for it is written, "*Cursed* be everyone who does not abide by all things written in the Book of the Law, and do them." (Gal. 3:8–10)

Note the contrast between the *blessings* associated with Abraham, and the *curses* associated with the law. Because the conditional cursing is the *new* element, Paul does not even mention the conditional blessings of the Sinai administration. Since blessings are common to both administrations (though the blessings of Abraham are unconditional, and those of Moses conditional), Paul does not even mention them. He mentions what is *distinctive* to the Sinai administration, in an effort to persuade Christians that they need not identify themselves as members thereof by circumcision. And, for Paul, the distinctive element is the conditional, temporal curse.[7]

Indeed, there is fairly good reason to believe that this is what the apostles referred to in Acts 15, when they debated in Antioch whether the Gentiles needed to keep the Mosaic law ("But some believers who belonged to the party of the Pharisees rose up and said, 'It is necessary to circumcise them and to order them to keep the law of Moses'"—15:5). Referring to this Mosaic law, Peter said, "Now, therefore, why are you putting God to the test by placing a yoke on the neck of the disciples that neither our fathers nor we have been able to bear?" (15:10). What was it that both the fathers and the Jewish Christians of the first century found unbearable about

7. I am aware that some think that Paul is discussing an abuse of the Sinai covenant, rather than the covenant itself. Such exegesis may be due to theological bias, however, since the text gives us three compelling reasons, each sufficient in its own right, to indicate that Paul is describing the Sinai covenant itself, and not some alleged abuse thereof. First, at 3:17, he refers to the "law" as that which came years after the promise. He manifestly refers, therefore, to the *inauguration* of the Sinai covenant itself, not some centuries-later abuse thereof. Second, as the passage cited demonstrates, the "curse" is not associated with an abuse of the covenant; Paul quotes Deuteronomy 27:26, indicating that this conditional curse-sanction is a part of the covenant *itself*. Thus, for Paul, the Sinai covenant introduces some new realities to the previously existing Abrahamic covenant, one of which is the threat of a temporal curse that hangs over Israel. Third, when he concludes his reasoning in this section with a figure of speech regarding Sarah (who represents the Abrahamic covenant) and Hagar (who represents the Sinai covenant), Paul says that "these women are two covenants. One is from Mount Sinai, bearing children for slavery; she is Hagar" (Gal. 4:24). In Galatians 3 and 4, Paul refers to the "covenant" that is inaugurated "from Mount Sinai," four hundred and thirty years after the Abrahamic promise. He is not discussing an alleged Jewish abuse of that covenant sometime later, but the terms of the covenant itself. For a further discussion, see T. David Gordon, *Promise, Law, Faith: Covenant-Historical Reasoning in Galatians* (Peabody, MA: Hendrickson Publishing, 2019), 108–64.

the Mosaic law? Was it the righteousness contained in it? Of course not; the way of righteousness is the way of life. Was it not the threats of cursing on Israel's disobedience that made the law of Moses an insufferable yoke? Was it not grievous for sinners to live in a covenant that threatened temporal sanctions on disobedience?

Therefore, any of the covenant-sanctions recorded in the Sinai covenant that describe temporal blessings or cursings that will attend Israel's obedience or disobedience are a distinctive element of that covenant administration, a distinctive element that we would not expect to carry over into the new covenant.[8] Thus, while Israel, if she were godly and obedient, could expect temporal blessings in this life, Paul suggests the faithful new covenant saint should expect just the opposite: "All who desire to live a godly life in Christ Jesus will be persecuted" (2 Tim. 3:12). When the Corinthians challenge his apostolic authority, he proves his call and faithfulness by recounting temporal cursings, not blessings:

> Five times I received at the hands of the Jews the forty lashes less one. Three times I was beaten with rods. Once I was stoned. Three times I was shipwrecked; a night and a day I was adrift at sea; on frequent journeys, in danger from rivers, danger from robbers, danger from my own people, danger from Gentiles, danger in the city, danger in the wilderness, danger at sea, danger from false brothers; in toil and hardship, through many a sleepless night, in hunger and thirst, often without food, in cold and exposure. And, apart from other things, there is the

8. An able discussion of the history of this question, and of the theological issues involved, can be found in Samuel Bolton's *The True Bounds of Christian Freedom* (1645). The Westminster Assembly may not have enjoyed unanimous consensus on this issue, and so its comment is somewhat cryptic. The Westminster Confession of Faith, chapter 19.6, says about the law, "The threatenings of it serve to show what even their sins deserve; and what afflictions, in this life, they may expect for them, although freed from the curse thereof threatened in the law." One could argue that the latter two clauses are in tension with each other. Shall we expect "afflictions, in this life" from disobeying the law, or are we "freed from the curse thereof threatened in the law"?

daily pressure on me of my anxiety for all the churches. Who is weak, and I am not weak? Who is made to fall, and I am not indignant? (2 Cor. 11:24–29)

New covenant believers expect to suffer with and for their suffering Redeemer. They intend to know him in the power of his resurrection and in the fellowship of his suffering, being conformed to the likeness of his death (see Phil. 3:10), and they accept that they are privileged by God's grace, "that for the sake of Christ you should not only believe in him but also suffer for his sake" (Phil. 1:29).

Summary

Every biblical law is governed by two things: the Creator's innate, morally praiseworthy, and unchanging moral *character*, and the Creator's *purposes* for particular creatures. Every law given by God is thus consistent with both his *unvarying* moral being and his *varying* purposes for various creatures. God's creational mandate for the swarming creatures (see Gen. 1:22), for instance, is different from his creational mandate for those made in his image (see Gen. 1:28), yet it is consistent with his unvarying moral perfection. Similarly, some of God's purposes for covenant Israel were different from his purposes for the patriarchs (though his purpose to redeem the fallen race in the second Adam was the same) and his purposes for the new covenant community. It was *consistent* with God's moral character to command David and Solomon to erect a temple as a place to offer sacrifices; it was equally *consistent* with his moral character to do away with this temple in the new covenant administration (see 1 Cor. 3:16–17). Again, the law *requiring* circumcision, and the apostolic mandate *refusing* its requirement, are both consistent with God's moral character, but they are not equally consistent with his purposes for his various covenant communities.

Therefore, one solution that almost certainly won't work (other than for purposes of fruitless argument) is to expect before investigation that Sinai commands are likely to be continuous with or discontinuous with the new covenant. Most dispensationalists, for instance, expect discontinuity between the stipulations of the Sinai covenant and those of the new covenant, while most theonomists do just the opposite, expecting continuity between the stipulations of the Sinai covenant and those of the new covenant. In my opinion, neither of these expectations is supported by a sound biblical theology or by the Protestant tradition. Rather, we should expect covenantal integrity. We should expect the stipulations of a given covenant to be well-integrated into the covenant itself. Insofar as particular commands reflect features that a certain covenant shares with other covenants, we would expect continuity with other covenants; but insofar as they reflect features that a certain covenant does not share with other covenants, we would expect discontinuity.

Questions for Discussion and Reflection

1. How does the secular world "borrow capital" from the biblical understanding of the law model?
2. Rightly understood, the law model should foster humility rather than pride and legalism. Why?
3. How does interaction with the other models prevent the law model from becoming a tool for promoting legalism?
4. What does it mean to see "covenantal integrity" between the stipulations of the Sinai covenant and those of the new covenant?
5. Consider a situation in your own life where the law model could help you work through a specific ethical question. Describe the situation below and explain how the law model provides values discernment.

Case Study

Return to your case study from the opening chapter and answer the following questions with it in mind.

1. What is helpful about viewing the situation through a law lens?
2. What aspects of the situation, if any, does the law model not seem to address?
3. Based on the law model, what decision(s) would you advise a person in this situation to make? Why?
4. Are you satisfied with how the law model addresses this situation? Why or why not?

4

THE WISDOM MODEL

What is the likely outcome of this decision?

Wisdom is a necessary complement to law (and to the other three models), if one is to live well. Indeed, it may be more necessary than law, because wisdom is the capacity to observe the true nature of things and, therefore, to understand what works and what does not. Had there been no fifth commandment, for instance, would a wise person not have learned that one's respect for parents and elders accords with the nature of reality? There are no biblical commands regarding the use of digital technologies; does this mean that every decision we make regarding such use is equally wise, productive, or humane? Therefore, the wisdom model helps us answer questions like the following: What is the likely outcome of doing or not doing this? Knowing what we know about the natural order or about human nature, what will likely happen if we do this or do that?

The Biblical Basis for the Wisdom Model

The wisdom model arises from the Bible's teaching regarding our created ability to discover the latent capacities and potentials of the created order, and, of course, from the biblical wisdom literature (such as the book of Proverbs), as well as the other, "pragmatic" instruction within the Scriptures, such as Paul's saying, "'All things are lawful for me,' but not all things are helpful" (1 Cor. 6:12; see also 10:23). In other words, within the realm of that which is lawful, not everything is equally helpful or edifying.

The Bible promotes our God-given abilities to observe and evaluate, and those who do not observe and evaluate are called "fools." The wisdom literature teaches us to learn from and raise questions about what we observe. It promotes what might be called "the contemplative life," a life of frequent reflection, a life that is increasingly impossible in a media-saturated environment where our tools constantly alarm and distract us.

The Wisdom Model and Human Nature

The wisdom model understands life to consist, ideally, in making wise choices moment by moment, day by day. The human is made in the image of a wise God, who, by wisdom, created all things (see Prov. 3:19). If we do not perceive the wisdom within the created order, we do not perceive that created order rightly, because God made the world via wisdom. We should therefore endeavor to see how this wisdom manifests itself in the natural realm. The human has the ability to observe, and to learn from observing, that choices have consequences. Some of these consequences accord with God's purposes and will; others do not. Some consequences contribute to health; others do not. Some consequences accord with the natural order; others do not.

These consequences should not be understood narrowly. While the wisdom model considers behavioral consequences, it also considers the natural order itself, a natural order that (ordinarily) has certain consequences that accord with nature.

For example, "a wise son hears his father's instruction" (Prov. 13:1). This will ordinarily have good consequences, because the father is older, more experienced, and more savvy than the son. But it is also right for younger people to honor and respect those who are older. The wise son does not merely calculate, in a narrowly pragmatic way, that his father's counsel is likely to be better than his own; he also recognizes that it is right to honor one's parents, even if the fifth commandment did not exist. A truly wise son does not, for instance, do his homework on a given evening merely because his father instructs him to do so; nor does he do so merely for the (consequentialist) reason that to do otherwise might bring punishment; nor does he do so because obedience might earn him better grades. A truly wise son recognizes that honoring his father is part of the very fabric of the social order that God created. It is right to honor one's father per se, apart from any other consequences. This is why "understanding" and "wisdom" are so frequently paired in the Scriptures (I found over forty examples):

And God gave Solomon wisdom and understanding beyond measure. (1 Kings 4:29)

Wisdom is with the aged,
    and understanding in length of days. (Job 12:12)

The fear of the LORD is the beginning of wisdom;
    all those who practice it have a good understanding.
        (Ps.111:10)

For the LORD gives wisdom;
    from his mouth come knowledge and understanding.
        (Prov. 2:6)

Blessed is the one who finds wisdom,
    and the one who gets understanding. (Prov. 3:13)

And the Spirit of the LORD shall rest upon him,
    the Spirit of wisdom and understanding. (Isa. 11:2)

It is he who made the earth by his power,
    who established the world by his wisdom,
    and by his understanding stretched out the heavens.
       (Jer.10:12)

And in every matter of wisdom and understanding about which the king inquired of them, he found them ten times better than all the magicians and enchanters that were in all his kingdom. (Dan. 1:20)

And so, from the day we heard, we have not ceased to pray for you, asking that you may be filled with the knowledge of his will in all spiritual wisdom and understanding. (Col. 1:9)

How the Wisdom Model Functions

The wisdom model makes possible honest differences in practice, because it recognizes that what works for one person does not necessarily work for someone else. Compared to the law model, for instance, the wisdom model is content with saying that some things (e.g., observing one particular day as religiously special [see Rom. 14]) are proper for one person to do and for another person *not* to do. Paul neither requires nor prohibits the observance of special religious days. It is neither "right" nor "wrong" in itself, and the decision to do it or to not do it will need to be made on other grounds. Some people have found that observing Lent is very helpful; others have never tried the practice or have tried it and found nothing helpful in it. Such differences are perfectly appropriate.

Similarly, some individuals have found the spiritual exercise of fasting to be very helpful, and they commend it to others on this ground. Others only find that it causes migraine headaches, and they eschew the practice. It is perfectly appropriate for such differences to exist. The practice of individual fasting, often promoted by students of the spiritual disciplines, should be distinguished from the fasting that is found in the Scriptures. With very few exceptions, the fasting recorded in the Scriptures is corporate, not individual (see Lev. 16:29–30), and it is often an element of national repentance on Israel's part (see Judges 20:24–26; 1 Sam. 7:6). Even on the rare scriptural occasion in which a fast is individual, it tends to be a penitential action performed by some important officer in the national covenant (for example, David's fasting for his son in 2 Samuel 12). Indeed, some of the Protestant confessions appear to acknowledge the public and corporate character of biblical fasting, such as the Westminster Confession of Faith, which refers to "solemn fastings, and thanksgivings upon special occasions" (21.5) as lawful elements of worship.

Additionally, the wisdom model, like the biblical wisdom literature itself, recognizes the paradoxical and ironic nature of life. Its instruction, therefore, would be contradictory, if taken as law. As an example, consider this: How should we answer a fool, when he speaks to us? Here's the wisdom answer to that question: "Answer not a fool according to his folly, lest you be like him yourself. Answer a fool according to his folly, lest he be wise in his own eyes" (Prov. 26:4–5). The wisdom model teaches us to consider the *effect* of our answer to "the fool." On the one hand, we don't, by our silence, wish to leave him "wise in his own eyes," thinking that his statement or worldview is true and reliable. But, on the other hand, we don't wish to adopt his manner and standard of reasoning (answering him "according to his folly"), lest we become foolish also. Taken as a *law*, then, this passage from Proverbs 26 is manifestly contradictory in its advice. Taken as wise *counsel*, there is no conflict at all.

Consider a few examples in which the wisdom model is necessary:

- Whether to marry or remain single.
- Whom to marry, and how to decide, if one chooses to marry.
- Whether to take a new job.
- Whether to go to college.
- What clothing to wear.
- Whether to purchase an automobile (and which one!).
- Whether and/or how much commercial media to consume (and which programs).
- Whether to exercise (and how, and how much).
- How to educate one's children, and to what degree.
- Whether to eat meat, drink wine, smoke, eat desserts, and so on (and whether to make such choices based on the constantly vacillating scientific studies or based on your own perception of how certain foods affect you).
- Whether to take a vacation (and where), or whether or when to retire from one's vocation.
- At what age, and under what circumstances, to permit one's children to date (I intend to be an open-minded parent here —when my daughters turn thirty, they may date whomever they wish).
- What kind of music to listen to.
  - Is it better to listen to artistically inferior music that is religious, or is it better to listen to artistically superior music, regardless of the composer's religious orientation?
  - Are there genres of music that should be avoided altogether, and if so, why?
- Whether to have unbelieving friends, and in what proportion to one's believing friends.

Note two things: most of these questions are unavoidable, and none of them can be answered by reference to biblical law. To be sure, one occasionally encounters individuals who think that some of the above can be answered through biblical law, but we are usually not persuaded that they have understood or applied the law correctly.[1] The fact is, we cannot answer many of life's most important questions (such as marital and vocational choices) by reference to biblical commands or mandates. Instead, we ought to answer these important questions by wisdom.

Where the wisdom model is not recognized, these important areas of life can only be addressed irreligiously. Indeed, for this very reason, we occasionally observe individuals or communities within the Christian tradition who attempt to find direction for such areas by other means: either by attempting to create laws where no biblical laws exist or by attempting to find answers to such questions by private revelation ("I think that God is leading me to take the job with General Electric"). Although we can appreciate people's attempts to organize and direct their lives by godly standards, we cannot approve their bypassing the ordinary way that God expects us to function: wisdom. The Scriptures urge us to "get wisdom" (Prov. 4:5; 16:16) because wisdom is such a necessary aid in life. If we repudiate God's scriptural counsel regarding wisdom, we cannot reasonably expect him to "lead" us by another means, as we have rejected the means he has appointed.

The tendency to assume that God will provide special direction is an understandable, though regrettable, error. It arises from reading those special occasions in Scripture when God *did* provide such guidance, with the (unnecessary) assumption that we should expect the same. Proof that such direction was exceptional, and not ordinary, comes from two different biblical lines of evidence.

First, in most of these occasions, the individual in question had some special function in the administration of God's covenant (e.g., he was a king, a prophet, or a priest). Thus, God "leads" Jonah by putting him in a large fish and taking him to Nineveh to prophesy.

---

1. See T. David Gordon, "The Insufficiency of Scripture," *Modern Reformation* 11, no. 1 (January/February 2002): 18–23.

Most of the rest of us use a Ford, or public transportation. And, if we genuinely thought that Jonah's situation were ordinary, then we would all sell our cars and wait for the next fish-taxi.

Second, there are manifest cases where God did not provide any such guidance, even where we might have expected it. Jesus commissioned the twelve apostles to preach, and he expressly warned them that if they went into a town or a house that didn't receive them, they should shake the dust off their feet and move on (see Matt. 10:14). And, as we read the book of Acts, we find that such dust-shaking occurs from time to time: "But they shook off the dust from their feet against them and went to Iconium" (Acts 13:51). Now, why wouldn't God have simply provided some kind of guidance to the apostles, so that they would have known where to preach fruitfully? And why are the decisions I face more important in God's economy than those of the apostles? Why would I expect special leading from God regarding my vocational decisions, when even the apostles didn't receive such direction?

I don't have opportunity here to enter the entire field of whether or in what manner such private leading occurs in the church age; my point is that the perceived *need* for this leading arises from a Christian subculture whose depreciation of wisdom has left us without any direction for making such decisions.

In one sense, the wisdom model functions before we answer a specific ethical question. That is, because wisdom is gained slowly and gradually, we cannot wait until we face a particular choice and then begin to develop wisdom. We must constantly, throughout our lives, be reflective, contemplative, and thoughtful. We must constantly speak with (even better: *listen* to) those who are older and/or more experienced or learned than us and be taught by them. We never know beforehand which of their observations, or our own, will equip us in the future to answer some specific question correctly.

Perhaps a counterexample would be apt. I met a Christian several years ago, who was roughly my age, a scientist by training, and an active churchman. As we chatted, he asked if I had been writing anything recently, and I indicated that I had nearly finished five hundred pages on Galatians, a book that grew out of my doctoral work over thirty years ago as well as my teaching the Greek text at graduate school and college for most of the time since then. He then took twenty minutes to explain the book of Galatians to me. I think the Scriptures have a four-letter word to describe such an individual, a word that begins with an "f" and ends with an "l."

There is another sense in which the wisdom model can function as we face specific choices. In such circumstances, the model tends to wrestle with the following considerations and questions.

Is there a choice to be made?

Every day of our lives, we make decisions—some weightier, and some lighter. Learning to be wise involves learning to make good decisions.

Does the Bible (especially the wisdom literature—Ecclesiastes, Proverbs, Job) address the matter generally?

Labor. Does the Bible address the issue of labor, before and after the fall (e.g., the mandate to exercise dominion over the created order, the mandate to cultivate the garden, the curse on labor)? Does the Bible commend or condemn sloth (see Prov. 19:15)? Does it commend working with our hands, so that we may have something to give to those in need (see Eph. 4:28)?

Human relations. Does the Bible provide general principles that govern marital (see Prov. 21:9, 19; 27:15; 1 Cor. 7; 11; Eph. 5; Col. 3; Titus 2; 1 Peter 3), parental and filial (Eph. 6; Col. 3), ecclesiastical (Heb. 13), or labor (Eph. 6; Col. 3–4; Titus 2) relations?

Child-rearing. Do the Scriptures teach any general principles about child-rearing? Which do the Scriptures commend more—self-expression or self-control (see 1 Cor. 9:25; Gal. 5:23; 2 Peter 1:6)? Do the Scriptures teach that children, apart from discipline and training, are naturally wise or naturally foolish (see Prov. 22:15)? Do the Scriptures teach that corporal punishment is always wrong or sometimes right (see Prov. 13:24; 22:15; 23:13–14)?

Food and drink. Are food and drink approved as gifts from God, to be received with thanksgiving (see Ps. 104:15; 1 Tim. 4:3)? Can one overindulge in food or drink (see Prov. 23:20–21; Eph. 5:18)? Are there other circumstances that might cause us to restrict otherwise lawful practices regarding food and drink (see Rom. 14; 1 Cor. 8)?

Human speech. Do the Scriptures condemn certain uses of human speech, such as talebearing (see Prov. 11:13), gossip (see Prov. 20:19; Rom. 1:29; 1 Tim. 5:13), or slander (see Prov. 10:18; Matt. 15:19; Rom. 1:30; Eph. 4:31)? Do the Scriptures teach that we should therefore always be silent or that we should use speech to heal rather than wound (see Prov. 10:31; 12:18; 15:2–4; 18:21)?

Does the nature of created reality commend one choice rather than another?

Is not the sexual difference between male and female biologically necessary for reproduction, for instance? Is this not part of our biological nature? Can same-sex sexuality lead to reproduction? To raise the question is to answer it; the human race will be able to "fill the earth" (Gen. 1:28) and exercise dominion over it only via opposite-sex unions. The commonwealth, therefore, has an interest in the union of man and wife through which other humans are brought into the world and reared to mature adulthood. It does not have the same interest in other unions and therefore need not protect such unions as it does opposite-sex unions. Same-sex unions are "contrary to nature," and they would be so even if Paul had not said as much in Romans 1:26.[2]

2. This does not necessarily mean that the commonwealth should criminalize such unions; it merely means that the commonwealth has no particular interest in preserving or protecting such unions.

Similarly, the Westminster Larger Catechism teaches that the commandment to "honor your father and mother" includes our submission to "all superiors in age and gifts."[3] It does so not because of any ordinary principles of biblical interpretation but because of the natural order; those who are less experienced or able should ordinarily submit to those who are more experienced or able. A budding carpenter should heed the counsel of an experienced carpenter if he wishes to build efficiently and safely. A less-experienced hiker should listen to the advice of a more-experienced hiker if she wishes to have a safe and pleasant time in the woods. Wisdom always seeks to understand the true nature of God's created order and to act in a manner that respects such order.

Who are the "multitude of counselors" from whom I can learn?

Biblically, "the fool" trusts in his own wisdom and opinion (see Prov. 26:5); by contrast, the wise distrust their own opinions and solicit the counsel of others (see Prov. 15:22). Genuinely wise people are *not*, ironically, "wise in their own eyes"; genuinely foolish people, ironically, *are* wise in their own eyes.

1. *Solicit a range of opinion.*
2. *Solicit opinions from people whom you know to differ on some matters* (for instance, someone who is more liberal and someone who is more conservative).
3. *Solicit opinions from people who are experienced in general* (i.e., "old"). You are not the first human to have lived, nor, ordinarily, the first to face a particular choice. Others have faced the choice, or similar choices, before.
4. *Solicit opinions from people who are experienced in the area in question.* For years, whenever I have planned some carpentry project, I have consulted with my father-in-law, who is an experienced carpenter. And, when I lived in

---

3. Westminster Larger Catechism, answer 124.

Massachusetts, I also would consult my former colleague at Gordon-Conwell, Doug Stuart, who is an accomplished carpenter. What is true of carpentry is true of many other tasks and questions in life. People who are more experienced in areas where we are less experienced may have important counsel. As a counterexample, don't solicit advice about child-rearing from people who don't have children. Why? For two reasons: First, people who don't have children will ordinarily render their opinion anyway, so you don't need to ask it. Second, and more seriously, they don't have any experience with child-rearing.

5. *Solicit opinions from people who are successful or who have recognized that they are unsuccessful.* You can learn from either person. One who has succeeded obviously learned something about the matter at hand, and, often, one who has failed has learned as much or more, provided one recognizes one's failure.

Are there "wisdom-sayings" in our language that might have elements of truth in them?

Benjamin Franklin was not inspired, but this does not mean that he was always wrong.

Are there patterns in human history from which we can learn?

This doesn't mean merely reading history books; it means being knowledgeable in a more general way.[4] One can learn more about human nature, for instance, from reading Shakespeare than one can from reading about the history of the Israelites (though one can learn a great deal about human rebelliousness by reading about the Israelites).

---

4. Though history books are quite helpful. See especially Barbara Tuchman's *The March of Folly: From Troy to Vietnam* (New York: Ballantine Books, 1985).

Are there patterns in your life from which you can learn?

Are there things you have done that have been successful (spiritually, physically, economically, familially, socially)? Are there things you have done that have been unsuccessful or unproductive?

Is the decision under consideration "timely"?

Wisdom raises questions such as the following: Which of the contemplated choices am I more likely to regret later? Which decision, though lawful in itself, is likely to be unsettling or disruptive (untimely) at the present moment? Which decision, if chosen, will constitute a lost opportunity?

The Westminster Standards are not deaf to this need for timeliness. Consider, for instance, Westminster Larger Catechism, answer 145, where the sins prohibited by the ninth commandment include "speaking the truth unseasonably, or maliciously to a wrong end." There are occasions when the truth not only *may* be properly withheld but also *ought* to be withheld.

Special Challenges to the Wisdom Model

Wisdom and the Dominance of the Law Model

In some evangelical circles, the dominance of the law model has virtually eradicated the wisdom model. In an understandable (and commendable) effort to guide life by biblical standards where the Scriptures speak, there has been an unnecessary tendency to depreciate the natural and human wisdom that God has given us as his image bearers. And where such wisdom is depreciated, it is less likely to be cultivated. As a result, we become less and less wise, rather than more and more.

Properly understood, an appreciation of human wisdom does not imply a depreciation of divine wisdom. Each has its own role in life, and each ought to be appreciated for what it brings to the table. Divine wisdom, where it is available, is always reliable, always right, and always trustworthy, whereas human wisdom must always be taken critically. Human wisdom may be right, or it may be wrong; insofar as it rightly observes the natural order, which God made "by wisdom" (Prov. 3:19), it still reflects on divine wisdom, just as biblical interpreters attempt to reflect wisely on God's revelation in Scripture. Human wisdom must understand Scripture well and perceive God's wisdom in the created order well, so the two enterprises are not as different as we often think. At any rate, human reflection on the divine wisdom by which the natural order was made is extremely valuable, and the Scriptures teach us to treat it as a precious commodity: "Wisdom is better than jewels, and all that you may desire cannot compare with her" (Prov. 8:11).

Wisdom and Technology

The depreciation of the wisdom model may also result from certain technological innovations. In oral cultures, everything one knows is received from real, living humans. In such cultures, it is very important to gather wisdom and to pass it along orally, that it may be remembered. Similarly, in such cultures, we learn to assess the *character* of the individual who is offering us advice. Is he the town drunk, the village idiot, the venerable saint? Is she modest and charitable, or wanton and debauched? The advice one receives, in oral cultures, always comes from an individual whose wisdom can be assessed.

The printing press changed this, and, until the invention of the telegraph, literacy became the primary means of learning. Literacy promotes learning by reading, and we read authors whose lives we do not necessarily know.[5] Protestants could become "people of the Book" only once we *had* a book, and, until movable type and inexpensive paper, believers didn't *have* any books. As we now evolve into

5. Indeed, the thesis of Paul Johnson's *Intellectuals: From Marx and Tolstoy to Sartre and Chomsky* (New York: Harper & Row, 1988), is that if we *did* know the life and character of people such as Shelley, Rousseau, Marx, or Tolstoy, we would not listen to a word they said.

a post-literate, image-based culture, it is difficult to predict whether wisdom will become more or less valuable to us.[6]

Electronic technologies also challenge those who would be wise because they frequently interrupt us. Telephones, smartphones, radios, televisions, and computers all compete for our attention (though few reward it). We are bombarded, all day long, with sounds, images, and slogans, all of which prohibit us from being alone with our own thoughts.[7] Various commercial interests compete for our "attention" (if you can call such distracted consciousness "attention"), and it takes resolve to refuse to grant attention to everything that claims it. The very nature of our high-tech culture militates against developing a concentrated attention span, and it will require conscientious, dedicated effort to exorcise the electronic demons from our personal environments.

Indeed, as Kenneth A. Myers has observed, communication technologies such as the cell phone permit those who are *not* present to interrupt our conversations with those who *are* present—they therefore prevent us from acquiring wisdom and the other benefits of human society.[8] Similarly, as C. John Sommerville has pointed out, commercial news broadcasts bombard our environments, attracting our attention to "current events," from which wisdom can almost

6. Students of orality will surely wish to consult Walter J. Ong, *Orality and Literacy: The Technologizing of the Word* (New York: Routledge, 1982); and Eric A. Havelock, *The Muse Learns to Write: Reflections on Orality and Literacy from Antiquity to the Present* (New Haven: Yale University Press, 1986). For general surveys of media ecology and the influence of media on social structures, one might consult Daniel J. Czitrom, *Media and the American Mind: From Morse to McLuhan* (Chapel Hill: University of North Carolina Press, 1982); Joshua Meyrowitz, *No Sense of Place: The Impact of Electronic Media on Social Behavior* (New York: Oxford University Press, 1985); Jack Goody, *The Interface between the Written and the Oral: Studies in Literacy, Family, Culture and the State* (London: Cambridge University Press, 1987); Gregory Edward Reynolds, *The Word Is Worth a Thousand Pictures: Preaching in the Electronic Age* (Eugene, OR: Wipf and Stock, 2001); Paul Levinson, *The Soft Edge: A Natural History and Future of the Information Revolution* (London: Routledge, 1997).

7. This is the thesis of Todd Gitlin, *Media Unlimited: How the Torrent of Images and Sounds Overwhelms Our Lives* (New York: Henry Holt, 2002).

8. Interested readers can learn more about this idea, and countless others like it, by listening to Mars Hill Audio, of which Ken Myers is editor. See https://marshillaudio.org/.

never be attained, while distracting our attention from reflections on history, from which wisdom can often be attained.[9]

Wisdom and Youth Culture

In the industrialized world today, wisdom is depreciated partly because we live in a youth culture: a culture that idealizes youth rather than age. Physical strength, athleticism, slender bodies, and non-gray hair (though any *other* hair color, even one that is foreign to the human species, is considered acceptable) are the ideals of a youth culture. Other cultures, especially Eastern cultures, have historically idealized age, with its concomitant wisdom. Indeed, one can hardly imagine a ninety-year-old Tibetan monk getting a facelift, a hairpiece, or Grecian Formula, for instance.

Tragically, youth culture idealizes that very moment of human experience (youthfulness) that the Bible characterizes as foolish. While we can hardly blame the youth for lauding youthfulness (they don't yet know how unwise and inexperienced they are), we can surely lament living in a culture in which so many *adults* idealize youthfulness. Our culture accepts the premise "no pain, no gain." It ought also to adopt the premise "no wrinkles, no wisdom."

Of course, my point is not that all youth are foolish, or that all older people are wise; to the contrary, "there's no fool like an old fool." My point is merely that youth culture will always tend to prefer those traits associated with youth to those associated with age. Youth culture will always tend to depreciate wisdom.

The Fast Pace of Life

If Western life is increasingly urban, and if urban life is increasingly fast-paced, such a pace will almost certainly militate against the attainment of wisdom. Wisdom requires not only observation (which takes time) but also reflection (which takes even more time).

---

9. C. John Sommerville, *How the News Makes Us Dumb: The Death of Wisdom in an Information Society* (Downers Grove, IL: InterVarsity Press, 1999).

Thinking about what one observes, and thinking about what others have said about what they have observed, requires uninterrupted time. It requires cultivating the ancient skill of sitting still, alone, without interruption of any sort, to think about life.

This skill cannot be acquired without great effort, because it will meet with stout resistance at every turn. Try sitting still, without a book in your hand or headphones on your ears, and see how long you can do it without others becoming nervous. People will stare at you, talk with you, ask you if you need help, offer you a ride somewhere, but they will not tolerate the sight of an individual sitting, alone, "doing nothing." It is intolerably countercultural. Indeed, I only indulge the practice myself by disguising it. When I wish to sit and reflect, I often put a notepad or a book in my lap. The book can be upside-down or written in a language I can't read; the notepad can already be filled up; but at least people aren't frightened that I am sitting alone, "doing nothing." They won't be upset if I read (though they will probably consider the practice quaint), but they cannot abide the sight of someone alone with his own thoughts.

An alternative ruse is walking. People in a fast-paced culture don't mind if you walk (though they look askance at sauntering and prefer a rapid pace, the gait of someone going somewhere hurriedly or "exercising"), so walking can be a socially acceptable way of reflecting. It permits one to be alone with one's thoughts, without the interruptions to thought that so characterize a hectic culture. And, as a final surreptitious means of being alone with your own thoughts, I recommend putting on a headset, even though you are listening to nothing (though, by all means, attach the headset to something digital, or you will surely be arrested or committed to a mental institution). This will lead others to think you are listening to something and will not alarm them with the frightening prospect that you are simply alone with your thoughts.

Whether wisdom, or its pursuit, will be permitted to complement the dominant law model, or whether it will survive the attacks of a hectic, technology-laden youth culture, I don't know, nor do I care to

predict. I do know that God would not have commanded the acquisition of wisdom if it were safe or right for us to live without it, so
I urge the reader to make every effort to acquire as much as possible.

Cautions about "Wisdom" Literature

The wisdom literature of the Bible is, of course, a wonderful
(though not exhaustive) source of wisdom, and it is well to reflect on
this literature frequently. However, one must be aware of the distinctive
features of this literature, or one may read it incorrectly. This literature
is designed to be memorable and practical. It does not ordinarily
intend to be exhaustive, but partial, and it is quite often paradoxical.
Four words of advice might help one understand it well.[10]

Wisdom Literature Provides Perspectives, Not Imperatives

Proverbs 14:7, for instance, says, "Leave the presence of a fool,
for there you do not meet words of knowledge." Now, taken as a
command, we would necessarily depart from the company of anyone
adjudged to be foolish by biblical standards. This would require us to
leave the presence of all unbelievers, whom the Scriptures describe as
foolish (see Ps. 14:1), yet we note that Jesus was often in the company
of tax collectors and sinners (see Matt. 9:10). This proverb provides a
perspective, a point of view. The point is that we should not expect to
find the highest degree of wisdom from a fool, and, therefore, when
searching for knowledge, we should go to wise and knowledgeable
people. As a perspective, it provides wise counsel. Misconstrued as
an imperative, however, it would mislead.

Since Wisdom Literature Is Often Partial, Read the Whole

The wisdom literature often reproduces foolish or vain perspectives on life and then comments on them. If we read the description

10. For a fuller treatment of this, see the excellent discussion in Gordon D.
Fee and Douglas Stuart, *How to Read the Bible for All Its Worth* (Grand Rapids:
Zondervan, 1981), 187–204.

of a given view but do not read the comment, we could take exactly the wrong point. Proverbs 9:17, for example, says, "Stolen water is sweet, and bread eaten in secret is pleasant." Contextually, however, we understand this to be the counsel of the "woman Folly," who "knows nothing" (9:13). And the following verse tells us about those who heed her advice: "He does not know that the dead are there, that her guests are in the depths of Sheol" (9:18).

Proverbs Are Neither Promises nor Legal Guarantees

Wisdom literature observes tendencies; it views the ordinary consequences of certain choices and the natural order that lies beneath them. But life is not always ordinary, and there are many exceptions to these observations. Therefore, when wisdom literature commends a certain behavior because of its typical consequences, it does not intend to suggest that such consequences will invariably follow. "Early to bed and early to rise makes a man healthy, wealthy, and wise" is a fine wisdom statement, and it rightly advises us to retire early in order to wake up early and get going. However, some people have better health than others, and Ben Franklin did not intend to suggest that this was a cure for tuberculosis. Further, there will always be some "night owls," who are simply more productive in the evening. Had Winston Churchill attempted to change his behavior to satisfy Franklin, rather than working until 3 a.m. or later (as was his custom), the Allied Powers would likely have lost the Second World War.

The same is true of biblical wisdom literature. Take, for example, Proverbs 15:1: "A soft answer turns away wrath, but a harsh word stirs up anger." This is not a promise, nor is it a legal guarantee. We may encounter people who are so angry that nothing we say or do will calm them down.[11] A soft answer is commended because of its *tendency* to avert anger and promote understanding, not because it always does so.

---

11. A police officer friend of mine was once called to the scene of a man in a cocaine-induced rage, and nothing but Mace would turn away his wrath.

Another example of this principle is even more disturbing, because it combines a suspicious translation with a belief that wisdom literature affords guarantees: "Train up a child in the way he should go; even when he is old he will not depart from it" (Prov. 22:6). Even if this translation were accurate, it would only indicate that there is a *tendency* for one's life to be shaped by its earliest days. The "habitus" of life is shaped from childhood; therefore, parents should beware of the importance of the early training a child receives. This does not guarantee, of course, that there are no exceptions, and it does not mean that if a child goes astray as an adult, this is the result of glaring parental failure.

Complicating this particular example is the fact that the original Hebrew text says nothing about "the way *he should go*"; it merely says, "Train up a child in his way," which might very well mean just the opposite of the common translation. Indeed, it might be ironic: "Let a child (in whose heart folly is bound—Prov. 22:15) go in his own way, and when he's old, he will still go in his own (foolish) way."[12] I think this is a better translation, but even here it is not a guarantee: it is a statement of a tendency. God's grace *can* win even someone who was never disciplined as a child, who was always permitted to have his own way.

Since Wisdom Literature Is Designed to Be Memorable, It Is Not Always Technically or Literally True

"The rich rules over the poor, and the borrower is the slave of the lender" (Prov. 22:7). The individual who borrows money for a

12. While the common translation is grammatically possible, I think it is profoundly unlikely. The reason is the use of the word "way" in the Bible, and especially in wisdom literature, where one's own way is so frequently spoken of as a grave mistake. See, for example, Proverbs 1:29–31: "Because they hated knowledge and did not choose the fear of the LORD, would have none of my counsel and despised all my reproof, therefore they shall eat the fruit *of their way*, and have their fill of their own devices." Similarly, "The way of a fool is right in his own eyes, but a wise man listens to advice" (Prov. 12:15). And of course, there is this familiar proverb: "There is a way that seems right to a man, but its end is the way to death" (Prov. 14:12; 16:25; see also 21:2). Therefore, "train up a child in his way" probably means "let a child go his own, undisciplined way."

conventional mortgage in the twenty-first century is hardly a slave to the mortgage banker, especially in a country where bankruptcy laws are so lenient. Borrowing places the borrower under obligation to the lender; therefore, borrowing should not be done lightly or inconsiderately. One should not over-encumber oneself with obligations, including monetary ones. This is the only point of the proverb.

The Commend/Command Distinction

One of the great benefits of the wisdom model is that it permits us to *commend*, in areas where we have no authority to *command*. The law model, properly used with a due consideration of the challenges inherent in applying biblical laws, permits us to command. Ministers and elders, who represent God, can command that people abstain from theft, murder, or adultery, by appeal to God's command. The wisdom model permits us to *commend*, on the basis of human wisdom, things that we have no authority to *command*, on the basis of divine revelation. If we find it helpful to read the Psalms, or the Bible generally, or some Christian hymns devotionally, we can certainly *commend* such practices to others, without obliging them to do so by *command*.

Evangelist and author Leighton Ford spoke with several of us over lunch some years ago, and he recommended reading five psalms and a chapter of Proverbs devotionally each day, by which method one could work through both books in a month. I have often followed this practice, and have found it helpful; the combination of devotional literature and practical literature is a great aid to private worship. Neither Leighton Ford nor I, however, would ever consider *commanding* such a practice—we are content to *commend* it.[13]

---

13. Indeed, I similarly commend the practice of reading the exposition of the Decalogue in the Westminster Larger Catechism. If you read the questions and answers for one "word" each day, you can cover the entire exposition thrice in a month. It contains a great deal of thoughtful material that is useful to consider at the beginning of the day. It can also disclose our sinfulness and make us grateful for Christ's atonement.

People frequently ask their pastors and elders for counsel, and some pastors and elders refuse to give any counsel until they have huddled together to determine whether the session has a "position" on the matter. This is a regrettable waste of an opportunity to offer advice. Often, the best thing for the individual is to get three *different* opinions, because the Scriptures teach that there is success in an "abundance of counselors" (Prov. 11:14; 24:6). A given church is under no obligation to have a position on matters not addressed in Scripture; indeed, it ordinarily should *not* have a position on extrabiblical matters. Yet her officers, as experienced and wise people, could help immensely by simply giving their own private opinion and counsel on the matter at hand. The "holy huddle" actually *prevents* people from acquiring wisdom biblically, because they either get no reply, or they get a single, homogenized reply, rather than the "abundant" counsel of a variety of perspectives.

When ministerial candidates occasionally preached at the church where I served as pastor, the elders adopted a wise practice. Three different officers were assigned, beforehand, to evaluate the sermon for the candidate. This provided the candidate with three *distinct* opinions about the sermon, rather than one homogenized opinion. A wise candidate would almost certainly have profited more from this range of counsel than he would have from a single, session-approved view.

Questions for Discussion and Reflection

1. What is unique about employing the wisdom model to an ethical dilemma, compared with the other models?
2. Which challenge to the application of the wisdom model affects you most?
3. In what way is the wisdom model's approach to ethical questions partly subjective? Do you find this subjectivity problematic or not? Explain your answer.

4. How does a proper understanding of the nature and genre of biblical wisdom literature help as we approach seemingly contradictory passages such as the following:

> Answer not a fool according to his folly,
>   lest you be like him yourself.
> Answer a fool according to his folly,
>   lest he be wise in his own eyes. (Prov. 26:4–5)

5. How are you currently cultivating wisdom in your life? Think of a person you know who is marked by wisdom. How might you emulate him or her?

Case Study

Return to your case study from the opening chapter and answer the following questions with it in mind.

1. What is helpful about viewing the situation through a wisdom lens?
2. What aspects of the situation, if any, does the wisdom model not seem to address?
3. Based on the wisdom model, what decision(s) would you advise a person in this situation to make? Why?
4. Are you satisfied with how the wisdom model addresses this situation? Why or why not?

5

THE COMMUNION MODEL

> *How might this decision enhance or inhibit my (or our)*
> *communion with God?*

The communion model understands human life to consist, ideally, in communication, discourse, or communion with God. The human is understood to have the unique ability, among creatures, of linguistic communication: of being able to address, and be addressed by, God. For the communion model, prayer is not something one does occasionally, in moments or seasons of special need. Life itself is prayer, a fellowship with God. Augustine introduced his *Confessions* with a quotation of Psalm 145:3, followed by this observation about man: "Man desires to praise thee, for he is a part of thy creation; he bears his mortality about with him and carries the evidence of his sin and the proof that thou dost resist the proud. Still he desires to praise thee, this man who is only a small part of thy creation. Thou hast prompted him, that he should delight to praise thee, for thou hast made us for thyself and restless is our heart until it comes to rest in thee."[1] Similarly, John Owen spoke of our life as one of communion with God:

> Our communion, then, with God consisteth in his *communication of himself unto us, with our returnal unto him* of that which he requireth and accepteth, flowing from that *union* which in Jesus Christ we have with him. And it is twofold:—1. *Perfect and complete*, in the full fruition of his glory and total giving up of ourselves to him, resting in him as our utmost end; which we shall enjoy when we see him as he is; and, 2. *Initial and incomplete*, in the firstfruits and dawnings of that perfection which we have here in grace, which only I shall handle.
>
> It is, then, I say, of that mutual communication in giving and receiving, after a most holy and spiritual manner, which is between God and the saints while they walk together in a covenant of peace, ratified in the blood of Jesus, whereof we are to treat.[2]

Note that Owen recognized a two-stage life of communion: initial and incomplete communion with God now; perfect and complete communion in the next life. Thus, in this life, the "rest" that Augustine spoke of will always include an element of "unrest." Our "rest" in God is imperfect now but will be perfected later. This present "unrest" is perhaps what led Blaise Pascal to observe, "All men's miseries derive from not being able to sit in a quiet room alone."

To be sure, we occasionally hear of individuals who claim to enjoy perfect communion with God, and indeed, there are even theological traditions that teach some form of "perfectionism," but most of us recognize that perfect communion with God awaits the life to come. Incomplete as our communion with God is, it is truly

---

1. Augustine, *The Confessions of St. Augustine,* trans. Albert C. Outler (1955). Available at https://faculty.georgetown.edu/jod/augustine/conf.pdf.
2. John Owen, *Communion with God,* ed. R. J. K. Law (Edinburgh, Banner of Truth, 1991), 9.

blessed, and we therefore ought to pursue it as fervently as we can. As a "model" for living, then, the communion model approves that which enhances our vital experience of life with or before God, and it disapproves that which damages this vital experience.

We might also note that Owen understood this communion to be a genuine, twofold reality, in which God communicates himself to us, "with our returnal unto him." This preserves the true dialogical nature of communion as well as the important reality that God initiates the dialogue. He not only creates humans with the capacity for communion with him but also addresses us, in various ways, inviting our reply to him.

Therefore, as we walk through life, making decisions and evaluating choices (the ethical program), we do so within a context that understands human life itself to be a life of communion with God. Decisions that enhance or contribute to this fundamental reality (for ourselves or for others) are superior to decisions that prevent or disturb this fundamental reality. Every choice we make in life is, as it were, a fork in the road, in which one path leads toward communion with God and another leads away from such communion. Thus, the communion model helps us ask the following question: Do our choices foster our communion with God, or do they detract from it?

Biblical Basis for the Communion Model

The communion model arises not only from this particular, communicative ability of the human race (we are *able* to communicate, linguistically) but also from the reality that God addresses us and teaches us to address him. Even after our first parents were banished from God's fellowship in the garden, God continued to address his people through prophets and through inscripturated revelation. And indeed, much of that revelation includes the requirement that God's people pray to him.

It is not surprising that Israel's life with God is recorded not only in the historical books of the Old Testament Scriptures but also in the collection of devotional literature, the Psalms. In these, we find an enduring record of the communication of God's people with him, through thanksgiving, lament, praise, and so on. Indeed, one could even argue that Adam and Eve's preference to communicate with the creature rather than the Creator led to all the woe our race has ever experienced. The Genesis narrative contains both God's and the Serpent's communications with Adam and Eve regarding the tree, and it is their "listening" to the voice of the Serpent, rather than to the voice of God, in which their sin essentially consisted. As the apostle Paul writes,

> Although they knew God, they did not honor him as God or give thanks to him, but they became futile in their thinking, and their foolish hearts were darkened. Claiming to be wise, they became fools, and exchanged the glory of the immortal God for images resembling mortal man and birds and animals and creeping things. Therefore God gave them up in the lusts of their hearts to impurity, to the dishonoring of their bodies among themselves, because they exchanged the truth about God for a lie and worshiped and served the creature rather than the Creator, who is blessed forever! Amen. (Rom. 1:21–25)

Accordingly, Paul instructs redeemed people to pray without ceasing, "giving thanks *always* and *for everything* to God the Father in the name of our Lord Jesus Christ" (Eph. 5:20; see also 6:18; 1 Thess. 5:16–18).

The Protestant Reformers, influenced by these realities, spoke of living *coram Deo*, "in the presence of God,"[3] recalling and reiterating Paul's teaching:

---

3. The expression is from Psalm 56:13 in the Latin Vulgate, about which Calvin said, "The words, *before God*, which are interjected in the verse, point to the difference between the righteous, who make God the great aim of their life, and the wicked, who wander from the right path and turn their back upon God." *Commentary on the Book of Psalms*, trans. James Anderson (1845; repr., Grand Rapids: Baker, 1975), 359.

None of us lives to himself, and none of us dies to himself. For
if we live, we live *to the Lord*, and if we die, we die *to the Lord*.
So then, whether we live or whether we die, we are the Lord's.
(Rom. 14:7–8)

This passage is one of the prooftexts for the remarkable first question
and answer of the Heidelberg Catechism.

The Communion Model and Human Nature

What follows is a brief overview of some of the biblical evidence
that suggests that life itself may be thought of as communion with
God and that therefore any attempt to evaluate life (the ethical task)
must consider whether a given choice contributes to, or detracts
from, this basic purpose.

Genesis 1–3; 11; 28

The creation account, and the narratives that immediately follow,
depict the human race as being distinctly made in God's image—we
are capable, therefore, of communicating with God. Indeed, some
theologians essentially define the "image of God" as the capacity to
relate to him.[4] God speaks to Adam and Eve in the garden, and even
after they revolt against his will and he banishes them, he continues
to address them, with words of judgment and promised redemption
(see Gen. 3:16–19). Communion with God has been greatly disrupted
by this curse-banishment, and it will not be reestablished in its ideal
form until the end of the age, when we shall see God (see 1 John 3:2).
Yet communion continues, albeit in a damaged and degraded form,
because to sever it entirely would be to destroy human life as such.
Perhaps this is part of what Paul intended in his words to Timothy:

---

4. See, for example, G. C. Berkouwer, *Man: The Image of God*, Studies in Dog-
matics (Grand Rapids: Eerdmans, 1962).

She who is truly a widow, left all alone, has *set her hope on God* and *continues in supplications and prayers night and day*, but she who is self-indulgent is *dead even while she lives*. (1 Tim. 5:5–6)

The curse-banishment is a harsh reality for those made in God's image, who are therefore capable of basking in God's presence. Revelation 21:3–4 promises its ultimate reversal:

And I heard a loud voice from the throne saying, "Behold, the dwelling place of God is with man. He will dwell with them, and they will be his people, and God himself will be with them as their God. He will wipe away every tear from their eyes, and death shall be no more, neither shall there be mourning, nor crying, nor pain anymore, for the former things have passed away."

Observe here that, when God reverses the banishment and dwells with humans again, he reverses the curses as well (no mourning, tears, dying, and so on). In between, however, humans suffer from the terrible reality that our created nature longs to fellowship or commune with God, yet we are banished from the blessedness that flows from his presence.

In Genesis 11, Moses recounts rebellious humanity's attempt to "storm heaven," as it were, by building a tower up to the heavens where God reigns, a tale that ends in divine judgment. In Genesis 28, however, what they longed for (and what we long for) is pledged to Jacob in his dream, in which he sees a ladder between heaven and earth, a highway of sorts that permits the angelic beings to ascend and descend, renewing communion between heaven and earth in a foretaste of Revelation 21. Until Jacob's dream becomes reality, all our communion with God is impoverished and partial; only when the last Adam completes his work will the blessedness of Revelation 21 appear.

Our longing for that endless moment when "the dwelling place of God will be with men" is undoubtedly what C. S. Lewis meant by the term *Sehnsucht*, which he called the inconsolable longing for "we know not what."[5] Well, at some level we do know what produces our inconsolable longing: our banishment from full communion with God. Despite every idolatrous effort to satisfy the desire for our Creator by worshipping his creation, it will not work; our longing for full communion with God will be fulfilled only in the next life. But even here, in the era of curse-banishment, God permits us to meet him by the special means he has appointed. He still addresses rebellious humans in various ways and allows us to address him.

God Communicates to Us

In the pattern of biblical communion, God, as our Maker and Lord, addresses us first, and we reply to his address. He addresses us through his creation; through special, linguistic revelation; and, most supremely, through his incarnate Son.

In some senses, God communicates to us through his creation. Theologians call this "natural revelation" (or, sometimes, "general revelation") because what God has made in the natural realm—which is therefore "generally" perceptible by all—reveals, or discloses, something about the nature of God. Paul said, "His invisible attributes, namely, his eternal power and divine nature, have been clearly perceived, ever since the creation of the world, in the things that have been made" (Rom. 1:20). He was articulating an old idea, one that was celebrated by the psalmist as well: "The heavens declare the glory of God, and the sky above proclaims his handiwork" (Ps. 19:1). Just as Rembrandt reveals something of himself in his paintings, and just as Brahms discloses himself in his music (he had great difficulty disclosing himself otherwise), so also God, the Originator of all creative activity, has revealed himself by what he has made.

God has also spoken specially and verbally to his covenant people through his Word and his sacraments. Theologians call this "special

5. For a thorough discussion of *Sehnsucht* in Lewis's writings, see Corbin Scott Carnell, *Bright Shadow of Reality: Spiritual Longing in C. S. Lewis* (Grand Rapids: Eerdmans, 1999).

revelation" because God does not reveal it to the entire human race; he only reveals it in a special manner to his covenant people. Indeed, Paul affirms that the special privilege of the Jews, in contrast with the other nations and peoples, was that God had uniquely disclosed himself to them:

> Then what advantage has the Jew? Or what is the value of circumcision? Much in every way. To begin with, the Jews were entrusted with the oracles of God. (Rom. 3:1–2)

God had given the sacrament of circumcision, the Levitical priesthood, the Passover meal, and his prophetic oracles not to the nations but to the Israelites. Indeed, the Israelites themselves were aware of this "special" privilege. As Moses said,

> For what great nation is there that has a god so near to it as the LORD our God is to us, whenever we call upon him? And what great nation is there, that has statutes and rules so righteous as all this law that I set before you today? (Deut. 4:7–8)

To the Israelites, by circumcision and Passover, and to the Christian church by baptism and the Lord's Supper, God has manifested himself to his people in a special way. Of course, these signs would be unintelligible apart from the linguistic revelation that accompanies them; therefore, his special revelation through sacraments has always been accompanied by special revelation through language.[6]

God's supreme disclosure of himself occurred when the eternal Son of God became incarnate and dwelt among us on earth.

> Long ago, at many times and in many ways, God spoke to our fathers by the prophets, but in these last days he has spoken

---

6. On the close relationship of Scripture and the sacraments, see Ronald Wallace, *Calvin's Doctrine of the Word and Sacrament* (Eugene, OR: Wipf and Stock, 1997).

to us by his Son, whom he appointed the heir of all things, through whom also he created the world. He is the radiance of the glory of God and the exact imprint of his nature, and he upholds the universe by the word of his power. After making purification for sins, he sat down at the right hand of the Majesty on high, having become as much superior to angels as the name he has inherited is more excellent than theirs. (Heb. 1:1–4)

Christ is compared to prophets and to angels because God had spoken to the world through prophets and angels—now, he has spoken supremely in his Son. Because Christ was such a revelation of God, John called him the "Word" of God:

In the beginning was the Word, and the Word was with God, and the Word was God. He was in the beginning with God. All things were made through him, and without him was not any thing made that was made. . . . And the Word became flesh and dwelt among us, and we have seen his glory, glory as of the only Son from the Father, full of grace and truth. (John 1:1–3, 14)

Jesus himself, in his incarnate state, was aware that he was the fullest disclosure of God that had ever been made. He therefore said to Philip, "Whoever has seen me has seen the Father. How can you say, 'Show us the Father'?" (John 14:9). Indeed, the Father is "glorified in the Son" (v. 13) precisely because the fullest revelation of God's character is manifested through the incarnation.

We Reply to God

Not surprisingly, when God addresses humans through his creation or through his Word and sacrament, he then calls the same humans to reply to him. Many biblical texts call us to verbally communicate with God (including all those texts that call us to "praise" or "thank" or "sing to" God).

1. *"Praying* at all times *in the Spirit, with all prayer and supplication"* *(Eph. 6:18)*. The original Greek reads, "Pray *in every season* in the Spirit." Paul's point is not that prayer can never be interrupted but that we are to pray in every *season*, or on every *occasion*, of life. We are to live all of life in God's presence and in the awareness of his presence. Joyous seasons of life are appropriate seasons for prayer; sad, frustrating, or discouraging seasons of life are also appropriate seasons for prayer, as are all the seasons in between. Every season of human life is a season for prayer, because human life is designed to be a life of fellowship with one's Maker.

2. *"Rejoice* always, *pray* without ceasing, *give thanks in* all circumstances; *for this is the will of God in Christ Jesus for you"* *(1 Thess. 5:16–18)*. Again, the point is not that one can never pause from praying to do something else, such as pay the bills or answer the phone. The point is that no event or circumstance, neither joy nor sorrow, pain nor pleasure, should be permitted to *interrupt* prayer or cause it to stop. Indeed, Paul says that "this is the will of God in Christ Jesus for you" because, to a great extent, God's will for the creature made in his image is for that creature to learn to commune with him in life's varying moments.

3. *"She who is truly a widow, left all alone, has set her hope on God and continues in supplications and prayers* night and day, *but she who is self-indulgent is dead even while she lives"* *(1 Tim. 5:5–6)*. Note the contrast: one "continues in supplications and prayers night and day," whereas the other "is self-indulgent." The latter widow, non-praying and self-indulgent, is "dead even while she lives." Human life so consists of "continuing" in prayers and supplication that those who do not live in such communion with God are described paradoxically as being dead even while they are alive. Those who do not commune with God the Creator, but rather indulge themselves with creaturely pleasures, don't really live.

The Communion Model

4. *"Is anyone among you suffering? Let him pray. Is anyone cheerful? Let him sing praise" (James 5:13).* Note that, whether suffering or cheerful, one communes with God—suffering should lead us to prayer, and cheerfulness should lead us to sing praise. Indeed, much of the challenge of our Christian pilgrimage consists in learning to do both. Some find it easier to commune with God when life is profoundly difficult but harder to do so when life goes well. For others, it is just the opposite. For all of us, the goal is to experience either suffering or cheerfulness in communion with God.

The Psalms

The entire Psalter testifies liturgically to a life in communion with God. Throughout the Psalms, Israel rejoices, thanks, laments, celebrates, and mourns. Whatever her life consists of, both pain and joy, she communicates with God. Indeed, it is instructive to note the prominence of laments in the Psalms. Of the one hundred fifty canonical psalms, over seventy of them—nearly half—are laments, while the other half of the psalms are divided into hymns of praise, thanksgivings, psalms of trust, salvation history psalms, and more. Thus, the lament is the most common category of psalm, proving that God permits and invites us to commune with him when life is challenging, frustrating, frightening, sorrowful, or perplexing.

This is profoundly significant for the history of religion, for human nature, and for the life of the covenant community. Most of the ancient Near Eastern religions were variations of nature religions: The peoples of the ancient Near East considered the sun (or some other aspect of nature, such as fertility) to be god, because the sun was the proximate source of so many earthly blessings (heat, vegetation, and so on). When "nature" frowned on such people, it was proof to them that they had displeased their deity. Similarly, in the Greek pantheon, many of the deities were believed to be capable of granting prosperity to humans who pleased them. In all of these religions, there was no ordinary place for piety or for communion with the deity when an individual or a people suffered.

Biblical religion challenges this entirely. Within the human race, all of which suffers due to God's curse on Adam and his descendants, there are those who are chosen to be God's people, and their suffering does not disprove that they are his people, nor does it put religion on hold. The prominent presence of lament in the Psalter proves that suffering need not be a barrier to communion with God, who tenderly and patiently listens to his grieving and suffering people. There is no reason to believe that suffering, confusion, disappointment, or sorrow disrupt our communion with God. We remain reconciled to him through the work of Christ, and he promises to sustain us in our needy moments.

Lament also challenges us to commune *with* those who suffer. Even a superficial reading of the biblical laments will convince the reader that not every Israelite was experiencing, on every occasion of chanting a given lament, the particular difficulty mentioned in the lament. Yet, in their corporate gatherings, the entire congregation chanted these psalms. Why? Because the non-sufferer identified sympathetically with the sufferer and permitted the sufferer's pain to be his, at least imaginatively so. His voice joined itself to the voice of the sufferer, breaking through the sense of loneliness that often attends suffering. One might even say that an Israelite never suffered alone—the covenant community lamented with him, and together, community and individual entered the presence of God, who welcomes those who are afflicted.

A Good Life, Unlike a Wicked Life, Is One That Is "Close to," "Near to," or "with" God

Noah was a righteous man, blameless in his generation. Noah walked with God. (Gen. 6:9)

When Abram was ninety-nine years old the Lord appeared to Abram and said to him, "I am God Almighty; walk before me, and be blameless." (Gen. 17:1)

Then Solomon stood before the altar of the LORD in the presence of all the assembly of Israel and spread out his hands toward heaven, and said, "O LORD, God of Israel, there is no God like you, in heaven above or on earth beneath, keeping covenant and showing steadfast love to your servants who walk before you with all their heart; you have kept with your servant David my father what you declared to him. You spoke with your mouth, and with your hand have fulfilled it this day. Now therefore, O LORD, God of Israel, keep for your servant David my father what you have promised him, saying, 'You shall not lack a man to sit before me on the throne of Israel, if only your sons pay close attention to their way, to walk before me as you have walked before me.'" (1 Kings 8:22–25)

For you have delivered my soul from death,
     yes, my feet from falling,
that I may walk before God
     in the light of life. (Ps. 56:13)

And the Lord said:
"Because this people draw near with their mouth
     and honor me with their lips,
     while their hearts are far from me,
and their fear of me is a commandment taught by men,
therefore, behold, I will again
     do wonderful things with this people,
     with wonder upon wonder;
and the wisdom of their wise men shall perish,
     and the discernment of their discerning men shall be
          hidden."

Ah, you who hide deep from the LORD your counsel,
     whose deeds are in the dark,
     and who say, "Who sees us? Who knows us?" (Isa. 29:13–15)

Jesus answered him, "If anyone loves me, he will keep my word, and my Father will love him, and we will come to him and make our home with him." (John 14:23)

But now in Christ Jesus you who once were far off have been brought near by the blood of Christ. (Eph. 2:13)

Note also that Paul's description of rebellious, fallen humanity in Romans 3:11 echoes the language of Psalms 14 and 15, when he says, "No one understands; no one seeks for God." For Paul, the fact that no one *seeks* for God is undeniable evidence of human corruption. To make sense of life, or to accept life, without seeking communion with one's Creator is the essence of fallenness and rebellion.

Psalm 73 as a Test Case

Psalm 73 follows the form of a lament psalm (some scholars consider it to be a wisdom psalm; if so, its wisdom lies in its observations about complaining and trusting). Typically, in a lament, the psalmist begins by candidly recording a complaint, which is ordinarily due to the oppression of the wicked. Ultimately, however, the psalmist acknowledges how impious it is merely to complain against God and his providence, and he then trusts in God. The first three verses of Psalm 73 thus set the stage:

> Truly God is good to Israel,
>   to those who are pure in heart.
> But as for me, my feet had almost stumbled,
>   my steps had nearly slipped.
> For I was envious of the arrogant
>   when I saw the prosperity of the wicked.

Verses 4–14 unpack the content of verse 3, as the psalmist contrasts the prosperity of the wicked with his own condition. The next major movement is found in verses 15–18:

If I had said, "I will speak thus,"
　　I would have betrayed the generation of your children.
But when I thought how to understand this,
　　it seemed to me a wearisome task,
until I went into the sanctuary of God;
　　then I discerned their end.

Truly you set them in slippery places;
　　you make them fall to ruin.

Note that the psalmist would have "betrayed" God's people had he merely complained. The turning point came when he "went into the sanctuary of God"; then he perceived "their end," and his own soul ceased its complaint. In the next few verses, he speaks more about the end of the wicked, and he rests in God's coming judgment. Then he says,

When my soul was embittered,
　　when I was pricked in heart,
I was brutish and ignorant;
　　I was like a beast toward you.

Nevertheless, I am continually with you;
　　you hold my right hand.
You guide me with your counsel,
　　and afterward you will receive me to glory.
Whom have I in heaven but you?
　　And there is nothing on earth that I desire besides you.
My flesh and my heart may fail,
　　but God is the strength of my heart and my portion forever.
For behold, those who are far from you shall perish;
　　you put an end to everyone who is unfaithful to you.
But for me it is good to be near God;
　　I have made the Lord God my refuge,
　　that I may tell of all your works. (vv. 21–28)

Note that the psalmist describes himself as "brutish" and "like a beast," as language and communication distinguish humans from other forms of animate life. Indeed, we once referred to other creatures as "dumb animals" because they were mute, incapable of discourse. But human life is essentially discursive; it is essentially social and relational, and above all relations is the relation to God. For the lamenting psalmist, the turning point came when he communed *with* God rather than merely complaining *about* God (or his providence). Once he went into the sanctuary, his mind changed.

The climax of the psalm is the conclusion, one of the greatest understatements in the Bible: "But for me it is good to be near God" (v. 28). Of course it is good for us to be near to God. We were created with the ability to commune with God, to rest in him and speak with him, to hear his Word and believe. Note the contrast in verses 27 and 28: there are those who are "far from" God and those who are "near God." All sin, therefore, is a turning away from God:

- We turn away from his praise and approval to seek the praise and approval of men.
- We turn away from his counsel to seek the counsel of men.
- We turn away from his comfort to find comfort in what God made.
- We turn away from his promises to attempt to secure our own wellbeing.
- We turn away from the noble pleasures he approves to pursue ignoble pleasures that he disapproves.

Any Christian ethical reasoning must wrestle with the reality that human life is designed to be a life of communion with God. Therefore, to properly evaluate life and its choices, we must consider communion. Do our choices foster communion with God, or do they detract from it?

How the Communion Model Functions

The communion model raises the following question regarding ethical decisions: How will the various options likely affect individual or corporate communion with God? Given the practices, environments, relationships, and activities that have enhanced communion with God in the past, how will the decision under consideration likely affect such communion? Given what Scripture or the Christian tradition has said about communion with God, how might the decision either enhance or diminish this communion? Given what we know about human nature and our own particular nature, how might the decision enhance or diminish communion with God?

Sometimes, in particular circumstances, the answers to such questions are fairly straightforward. On the one hand, suppose that someone is considering a job change. The current job is located in a good community where the family enjoys a very edifying church experience, while the alternate job is located in a community where there is no strong church. In all likelihood, communion with God will suffer if the family moves. On the other hand, another individual in the same circumstance, with an aptitude for church-planting, might deliberately move to the area that needs a strong church, in order to help plant one. In either case, however, the decision requires one to consider individual and corporate communion with God as well as the role of the visible church in such communion.

Other questions about labor and leisure may be less straight-forward, but we still ought to approach them with the communion model in mind. If, for instance, prayer takes great concentration, energy, and effort, what would be the likely effect of taking a job that required one to work seventy to eighty hours a week, commute included? The likely effect would be weariness, as the job and the commute would leave only a certain amount of time for various household duties, after which one would have a small amount of unwearied time (if any) for prayer, meditation, reflection, or reading. Many have observed the hectic and stressful nature of twenty-first-century American culture and have called attention to its consequences for physical and familial health. Fewer have observed that the same realities diminish communion with God.

Leisure issues are no less significant than labor issues. The use of our "free" time either contributes to or detracts from a life of communion with God. Certain activities open the mind and the soul to religious and spiritual concerns and cultivate a spirit of thoughtfulness and reflection, whereas others do not. Some years ago, for example, when I decided to learn to read poetry, I discovered (not immediately) that when I had read poetry for about half an hour, all of my sensibilities and knowing faculties were more alert; I noticed more, observed more. Further, I became more reflective and meditative, and I found that it was quite easy to move from poetry reading to prayer, especially prayers of wonder, praise, and thanksgiving. Although I did not expect poetry reading to have this effect on me, it did so anyway. Knowing this, I now consider poetry reading to be a good use of my leisure time. Many years earlier, I had had a similar experience with hiking and backpacking. I find that when I'm in the woods or the mountains, especially when I'm alone (but not only then), my soul is less distracted, the buzz of the inconsequential diminishes, and I notice, enjoy, and give thanks for God's work of creation.

Raising such questions about labor and leisure provides an additional perspective for decision-making. Interestingly, however, the answers to these questions are somewhat subjective (and therefore relative). I've taken some people hiking with me who, far from being moved to prayer, may have been moved to cursing! What is a lively, stimulating experience for me is a hellishly grueling experience for others; therefore, not everyone will enjoy enhanced communion with God through hiking. Each of us, however, should have little difficulty listing five leisure activities that tend to enhance our communion with God and five that tend to diminish it. In fact, we should have little difficulty listing our "top ten" leisure activities and ranking them, from one to ten, in terms of how they appear to affect our communion with God. Here's a sample list of leisure activities that, as far as I can tell, enhance or diminish my own communion with God.

Enhance Communion	Diminish Communion
Reading Frost's poems	Reading Spurgeon's sermons
Listening to Brahms	Listening to Contemporary Christian music
Conversing	Chattering
Hiking	Shopping

The purpose of such a list is neither to promote it nor to defend it; it may be that my choices reflect unusual perversity or depravity on my part. However, even if I am unusually perverse or depraved, it is still I, perverse and depraved as I am, who am called to commune with God. And if certain leisure choices enhance that communion for me, then for me they are better choices than their alternatives.

I still don't understand, for instance, why I rarely find it edifying to read Spurgeon's sermons, since others are so helped by this activity. Perhaps it is because a good sermon is designed to be heard, not read—in any case, reading "Birches" by Robert Frost is more likely to inspire prayer in me than reading a sermon by Spurgeon (a consequence that would probably irritate both Frost and Spurgeon). Similarly, it may not make sense that listening to contemporary Christian music merely irritates me, whereas listening to Brahms, who was no friend of orthodox Christianity, frequently moves me to prayers of thanksgiving. But it is less important to make sense of such experiences than it is to make wise choices among them, and for me, the list above reflects my current preferences, preferences that could change at any time.

If this book were about premarital counseling, I would now raise the question of what kinds of *homes* promote communion with God and what kinds do not. I am not speaking architecturally here (though architecture is profoundly influential)—rather, I am referring to the character or personality of the home and its effect on communion. What's true of people is often true of homes: some are loud, some are quiet; some are active, some are sedate; some are gregarious, some are shy. Which is more likely to promote communion with God: House A, in which there are several televisions and speakers playing, and people yell to each other from various rooms and floors of the house, or House B, in which those who listen to music use headphones, there are no televisions, and all conversations are held in the same room? I think the question, once raised, answers itself.

Therefore, when you ask whether to have a television (or several) in your home, you should consider the effect it will have on communion with God. When you ask whether to walk downstairs to speak with someone or whether to shout from where you are, you should consider the effect that might have on someone else in the home who is praying or meditating. Many homes are now architecturally "open," featuring rooms that open to other rooms. I tend to like these homes, aesthetically, when I visit or tour them. I suspect, however, that they (at best) enhance human communion at the expense of divine communion.

Raising such questions makes people nervous, partly because it puts them on untraveled ground and partly because it sounds as though I'm judging their choices. Actually, I think the answers to these questions are, ordinarily, relative rather than absolute. Just as I do not (and cannot) justify my preference of Frost to Spurgeon, I do not and cannot demand that only certain architecture and certain domestic practices are consistent with a life of communion with God. I can and do, however, raise the question, because the question is both pertinent and important. Many people who wish they lived in closer communion with God have unwittingly created an environment in which such communion can scarcely take place.

For my last eighteen years before retirement, each fall I taught an introduction to media ecology,[7] and my readings in this area have persuaded me that some technologies are likely to diminish human communion with God (and with other humans, for that matter). When I was a child, for instance, very few devices had alarms: the alarm clock obviously did, as did the telephone, and the oven had a timer with an alarm. As an adult, however, I am surrounded by alarms: my computer "alerts" me to incoming email; my smartphone alerts me about upcoming appointments or incoming text messages. And some of these technologies (unlike the oven or a traditional landline telephone) travel with me, so their alarms are more difficult to evade. But does not my communion with God require some uninterrupted silence? Can I pray or meditate when I am frequently interrupted or alarmed? Should I not make some self-conscious decisions about my use of such technologies if I wish to bolster my communion with God?

Consider again Blaise Pascal's comment: "All men's miseries derive from not being able to sit in a quiet room alone." Pascal was writing in the mid-seventeenth century, in a culture that was substantially less hectic than ours. In the literal sense of the word, nothing "alarmed" Pascal. Quiet rooms were at least available to his culture, even if people did not avail themselves of them. But for our culture, Pascal's coveted quiet room is an endangered architectural species. The inability he lamented was the lack of *desire* to sit in a quiet room; in our day, we ought to lament the near impossibility of *finding* such a room, even if one desired it. But communion with God requires some degree of quiet, and cultivating an environment that permits or prohibits such quiet will become an increasingly important dimension of the ethical task.

7. The term *media ecology* was apparently coined by Marshall McLuhan but was made more widely known by his protégé, Neil Postman, especially through Postman's *Amusing Ourselves to Death: Public Discourse in the Age of Show Business* (New York: Viking, 1985). As the name suggests, the discipline studies human environments, or ecologies, by observing the presence or absence of certain media on human behavior. Interested readers may consult the website of the Media Ecology Association here: www.media-ecology.org.

Special Challenges to the Communion Model

One particular challenge of the communion model is subjectivity. While there are some devotional activities that the church has found to be beneficial across the ages (e.g., prayer, Bible-reading), we are probably not very good judges of our own souls and selves. We must experiment to find practices that are more beneficial to us than others. Further, our cultural moment is very different from that of Blaise Pascal. In his seventeenth-century moment, before steam engines, large factories, or electricity, a quiet room could be found (though few entered it); in our moment, noise is nearly ubiquitous. I spend twenty or thirty nights annually hammock camping alone in a local state forest, and while I do not always find the practice especially edifying, it is quiet, and it affords an opportunity for thoughtful reflection and prayer.

Questions for Discussion and Reflection

1. In contemporary Western culture, few have a natural disposition toward contemplation and stillness. Name some of the challenges you face in creating a truly quiet environment.
2. What, if any, decisions are you currently considering in which you need to employ the communion model to prioritize time with the Lord in his Word and in prayer?
3. Was there a method of responding to or communing with God that you read about in this chapter that was new or unfamiliar? (Methods included praise, lament, rejoicing, and supplication.)
4. How does the communion model conflict with a legalistic lifestyle?

Case Study

Return to your case study from the opening chapter and answer the following questions with it in mind.

1. What is helpful about viewing the situation through a communion lens?
2. What aspects of the situation, if any, does the communion model not seem to address?
3. Based on the communion model, what decision(s) would you advise a person in this situation to make? Why?
4. Are you satisfied with how the communion model addresses this situation? Why or why not?

6

THE WARFARE MODEL

In the often invisible, yet real warfare between the forces of good and evil, will this decision likely serve the forces of good or the forces of evil?

Beneath everything else recorded in biblical history is the great warfare between Satan, God's rebellious creature, and God himself. Satan is malevolent, attempting to destroy all true pleasure, health, happiness, and holiness. God is benevolent, ultimately establishing in his created order the richest pleasure, health, happiness, and holiness. As early as the third chapter of Genesis, even as God cursed the created order because of Adam's sin, he also promised that there would be a great war in which God's purposes would triumph:

> The LORD God said to the serpent, "Because you have done this, cursed are you above all livestock and above all beasts of the field; on your belly you shall go, and dust you shall eat all the days of your life. I will put enmity between you and the woman, and between your offspring and her offspring; he shall bruise your

head, and you shall bruise his heel." (Gen. 3:14–15) (The word translated "bruise" here is rare, but in Job 9:17 it is translated as "crush," which may be more indicative of a serious wound than "bruise.")

Some may be uncomfortable with it, but one of the most common titles for God in the Bible, used 259 times, is "Lord Sabaoth," meaning the Lord of Hosts or the Lord of Armies. The title refers to God as he wages terrifying (and ultimately triumphant) war against his enemies and the enemies of his people. As a benevolent sovereign, he will not permit those who revolt against his reign to destroy the inhabitants of his realm, and he therefore wages warfare against the revolutionaries. While much of God's activity as Divine Warrior occurs in the context of geopolitical Israel, this is nothing less than a type of his eschatological warfare, anticipated in Genesis 3 and consummated in the realities recorded in the book of Revelation.

The Biblical Basis for the Warfare Model

The warfare model arises essentially from three streams of Scripture. First, the Old Testament's typological expectations of the coming of Christ often include military kings, who lead the people of God in triumph over their enemies. Second, there are those various "apocalyptic" passages in the Bible that describe the entire drama of human existence as a great war between good and evil, between light and darkness.[1] Third, there are those many passages that employ military figures of speech to describe Christian ministry, life, and duty:

> For though we walk in the flesh, we are not waging war according to the flesh. For the weapons of our warfare are not of the flesh but have divine power to destroy strongholds. (2 Cor. 10:3–4)

1. For example, "Then the dragon became furious with the woman and went off to make war on the rest of her offspring, on those who keep the commandments of God and hold to the testimony of Jesus" (Rev. 12:17).

Put on the whole armor of God, that you may be able to stand against the schemes of the devil. For we do not wrestle against flesh and blood, but against the rulers, against the authorities, against the cosmic powers over this present darkness, against the spiritual forces of evil in the heavenly places. Therefore take up the whole armor of God, that you may be able to withstand in the evil day, and having done all, to stand firm. (Eph. 6:11–13)

What causes quarrels and what causes fights among you? Is it not this, that your passions are at war within you? (James 4:1)

Beloved, I urge you as sojourners and exiles to abstain from the passions of the flesh, which wage war against your soul. (1 Peter 2:11)

Apocalyptic Warfare in the Bible

Scripture often employs military images when describing the future, final consummation of history. In these passages, God is envisioned as a great warrior, ultimately triumphing over the enemies who have despoiled his land, in order to restore order, justice, health, and peace (see Rev. 19:11–21). There is even a vision of warfare in heaven, as Michael and his angels make war against the dragon and his angels (see Rev. 12:7). The beast wages war against the Lamb of God (see Rev. 17). And the exalted Christ himself threatens to war against those within the churches who teach the doctrines of the Nicolaitans (see Rev. 2). In these visions, we perceive the utter incompatibility between righteousness and wickedness, between submission to God and resistance to his reign.

Military Descriptions of the Christian Ministry and the Christian Life

In light of these realities, it is not surprising that the New Testament often describes the Christian ministry and the Christian life using military language. Those who follow Christ are engaged in the great, historic warfare between life and death, health and illness, good and evil, justice and injustice. The Christian ministry is described in military terms; many passages describe the particular nature of Christian warfare and use martial language to depict the life of believers.

For example, in Philippians 2:25, 2 Timothy 2:3–4, and Philemon 1:2, Paul refers to ministers as soldiers. In 1 Timothy 1:18, he uses military language to describe Timothy's work:

> This charge I entrust to you, Timothy, my child, in accordance with the prophesies previously made about you, that by them you may wage the good warfare.

Certain texts describe the nature of this warfare. In Jesus's day, Hades was considered a place of torment in which souls were imprisoned. When Jesus told Peter, "On this rock I will build my church, and the gates of hell [Hades] shall not prevail against it" (Matt. 16:18), he was describing the church as a militant institution that breaks down the prison walls of Hades and releases its captives. Additional texts elaborate on this ecclesial conquest:

> As servants of God we commend ourselves in every way: by great endurance, in afflictions, hardships, calamities, beatings, imprisonments, riots, labors, sleepless nights, hunger; by purity, knowledge, patience, kindness, the Holy Spirit, genuine love; by truthful speech, and the power of God; with the weapons of righteousness for the right hand and for the left. (2 Cor. 6:4–7)

> Though we walk in the flesh, we are not waging war according to the flesh. For the weapons of our warfare are not of the flesh but have divine power to destroy strongholds. We destroy arguments and every lofty opinion raised against the knowledge of God, and take every thought captive to obey Christ. (2 Cor. 10:3–5)

Not surprisingly, the New Testament often describes the life of faith in military terms, depicting believers as soldiers who fight on one side of a great war.

> Do not present your members to sin as instruments [or "weapons"] for unrighteousness, but present yourselves to God as those who have been brought from death to life, and your members to God as instruments for righteousness. (Rom. 6:13)

The word translated "instrument" (*hopla*) ordinarily refers to military armament of some sort. Indeed, in contemporary English, we refer to a person who is afraid of guns as a *hoplophobe*. The term means "weapon" or "armor" in texts such as John 18:3, Romans 13:12, and 2 Corinthians 10:4.

In Galatians 5:17, Paul writes, "The desires of the flesh are against the Spirit, and the desires of the Spirit are against the flesh, for these are opposed to each other, to keep you from doing the things you want to do." The word translated "are opposed to" in this verse is commonly employed in martial contexts, to refer to one's "opponents" in warfare. Indeed, the devil himself is referred to by this term in 1 Timothy 5:14: "So I would have younger widows marry, bear children, manage their households, and give the *adversary* no occasion for slander." So the term is used in 2 Samuel 8:10: "Toi sent his son Joram to King David, to ask about his health and to bless him because he had *fought* against Hadadezer and defeated him, for Hadadezer had often been *at war* with Toi."

Other passages—such as Ephesians 6:10–17 (the armor of God), 1 Timothy 6:12, James 4:1–2, and 1 Peter 2:11—envision the Christian life as one of perpetual warfare, in which the forces of evil assault and oppose the forces of good, and vice versa. To believe in Christ requires us to enlist in his cause, to wage war against sin, and to resist its attacks on ourselves, the church, and human society. Not surprisingly, the 1928 Book of Common Prayer published by the Episcopal Church, following many similar vows in earlier liturgies, includes this question as part of its baptismal rite: "Dost thou, therefore, in the name of this Child, *renounce the devil and all his works*, the vain pomp and glory of the world, with all covetous desires of the same, and the sinful desires of the flesh, so that thou wilt not follow, nor be led by them?" Note the militant nature of this baptismal vow, some form of which can be found in Tertullian, Hippolytus, and Cyril of Jerusalem. Such vows imply that the baptizand is leaving the life of a citizen and beginning the life of a warrior.

Further, these passages often refer to the cosmic warfare as "resistance" on the one side or the other. Satan and his adversaries (including most of the structures of fallen human societies) "resist" the purposes and ways of God, and God's soldiers resist the resistance. To be a follower of Christ, one must be willing to spot resistance to God's rule and to resist such resistance. The entire force of well-known texts such as Romans 12:2 suggests this resistance: "Do not be conformed to this world, but be transformed by the renewal of your mind." "This world" is hostile to God's created purposes, and its various cultural expressions always manifest the resistance in their own peculiar ways. We must not be conformed to such resistance.

How the Warfare Model Functions

Before I discuss the duties of the Christian warrior, I must make an important qualification. The Christian faith and the Christian life cannot be reduced to a technique. Jacques Ellul and David F. Wells[2] have made this case cogently. We need the grace of the Holy Spirit either to enter this warfare or to make any headway therein, and even as we consider those practices, disciplines, and duties by which soldiers wage holy warfare, we must do so with a due recognition that there can be no progress whatsoever apart from the blessings of the Ascended Christ, chief of which is his gift of the Holy Spirit. Only

2. See Jacques Ellul, *The Technological Society*, trans. John Wilkinson (New York: Knopf, 1964); and David F. Wells, *No Place for Truth: or Whatever Happened to Evangelical Theology?* (Grand Rapids: Eerdmans, 1993).

the last Adam, the Seed of the woman, can emerge victoriously over the seed of the Serpent, and all smaller sub-victories are part of his great work, both in his humiliated state and in his exalted state. So we undertake this warfare as a minister undertakes preaching: with complete dependence on the work of Christ and his Spirit.

Watchfulness

One of the most common, universal duties in any military is that of the watch. Since surprise is one of the great tactical assets of every army, watchfulness is, and always has been, an essential element of warfare. In ancient times, the watch was quite literally visual; in more recent times, it also includes radar, sonar, satellite photography, and electronic eavesdropping. But the mission has remained the same: don't let the enemy sneak up on you and catch you unprepared. Many biblical texts warn us to adopt the same strategy. Peter urged us, "Be sober-minded; be watchful. Your adversary the devil prowls around like a roaring lion, seeking someone to devour" (1 Peter 5:8).

Obedience to Orders

Similarly, obedience is a universal aspect of military life, whether ancient or modern. There may be a place for developing a philosophy or theology of warfare and for debating such things as just war theory, but the battlefield is not that place. Once an engagement has begun, everyone must respect the chain of command, and all inferiors must obey the commands of their superiors.

> But the centurion replied, "Lord, I am not worthy to have you come under my roof, but only say the word, and my servant will be healed. For I too am a man under authority, with soldiers under me. And I say to one, 'Go,' and he goes, and to another, 'Come,' and he comes, and to my servant, 'Do this,' and he does it." When Jesus heard this, he marveled and said to those who followed him, "Truly, I tell you, with no one in Israel have I found such faith." (Matt. 8:8–10)

In some sense, then, we might suggest that the warfare model embraces the law model, because the obedience that is such a prominent feature of the law model is also a necessary component of the warfare model.

Equipment and Preparation

Students of the Second World War are quick to point out that American industrial might was critical to the Allied victory. The Americans surprised the Japanese by the speed with which they rebuilt the Pacific Fleet after Pearl Harbor, and Hitler could not compete against the ships, airplanes, tanks, and landing craft that the United States produced with great efficiency. The cost of equipping soldiers has increased considerably in the last half century or so: in WWII, it was $170 per soldier; in the Vietnam War, $1,112; and in more recent operations, it is $17,472, primarily because of the rising cost of body armor, communications, and sighting equipment (day and night) for weaponry.[3] An ill-equipped army cannot defeat a well-equipped one—many battles are won before the first round is fired, because of the successful equipping and preparation that precede the battle itself.

Similarly, in the Scriptures, believers are instructed to prepare and equip themselves for war by putting on the entire armor of God (Eph. 6) and by arming themselves with the right kind of weapons (2 Cor. 10:3–6).

Strategy—Offensive and Defensive

In any military engagement, the highest-ranking officers deliberate and develop strategies, and these strategies are both offensive and defensive. Offensively, the officers determine where and by what means they might achieve the greatest victories; defensively, they determine where their greatest weaknesses lie and how to defend these areas against attacks. Where would a successful offensive

3. Associated Press, Thursday, October 4, 2007.

procure a great victory? Where would a defeat prove a real setback? Where is the enemy weak? Where am I weak?

Believers must think strategically as well. We must develop long-range offensive strategies—plans to make progress and take ground that is not currently ours. We must also consider defensive strategies, honestly assessing our own personal, ecclesiastical, and cultural weaknesses that the Enemy might exploit, and striving to prevent such victories.

Knowledge of the Enemy

The apostle Paul told the Corinthians,

> What I have forgiven, if I have forgiven anything, has been for your sake in the presence of Christ, so that we would not be outwitted by Satan; for we are not ignorant of his designs. (2 Cor. 2:10–11)

Sadly, in our present day, we are almost entirely "ignorant of his designs." If I were to give a pop quiz and say, "Name five of Satan's designs," how many would pass? How often do we familiarize ourselves, through study and conversation, with Satan's designs? Of course, we know that he tries to break our communion with God; we know that he tempts us to sin. But do we know *how* he goes about breaking that communion or *how* he goes about tempting us to sin? If we don't, then we are ignorant of his designs, at our own peril.

As an example, consider Satan's designs in our contemporary high-tech culture. What does Satan desire but to disrupt our communion with God? And how might our culture and its tools aid him in his effort? Well, in a "connected" culture—where social media, texting, video calling, voicemail, and email are ubiquitous—doesn't such increased communication with humans naturally result in decreased communion with God? It isn't easy today to find a place where one can be alone and undisturbed; our technologies, unless we deliberately turn them off, prevent us from having uninterrupted seasons of prayer and meditation. We must not be ignorant of the ways in which Satan would use these tools, and we must intentionally use them in a manner that enhances our true communion with God and with others.

Special Challenges to the Warfare Model

Satan's Weapons: Deceit and Desire

Scripturally, we find again and again that the primary weapons in Satan's arsenal are deceit and desire (especially strong desire, or passion). When Satan deceives our understanding, we then behave in a manner consistent with that deception. He makes the world look a certain way to us, and we then behave in accordance with that perception of the world. Of course, the perception is wrong, and the behaviors that follow are destructive. Jesus said about him, "You are of your father the devil, and your will is to do your father's desires. He was a murderer from the beginning, and does not stand in the truth, because there is no truth in him. When he lies, he speaks out of his own character, for he is a liar and the father of lies" (John 8:44).

Satan deceived Adam and Eve into thinking that God's purposes for them were malicious and would prove harmful. He deceived them into thinking that it was better and wiser to follow him (the Serpent) than God. Once they were so deceived, they behaved accordingly. This remains the preeminent deception Satan employs today. He always attempts to deceive us into thinking that God is malevolent, and that following God will ruin our lives, when nothing could be further from the truth. Following Satan (and his close cousin, self) debases us, demeans us, dehumanizes us; it cuts us off from that great pleasure of knowing and serving God and neighbor—a pleasure that ennobles us and humanizes us—and it substitutes fleeting, debasing pleasures for lasting, ennobling pleasures.

Satan deceives us into thinking that life is better if we seek our own will; the truth is that life is better—both for us and for those around us—if we deny our will and seek God's. Satan deceives us into thinking that God doesn't care for us, which leads us to worry and despair; the truth is that God cares for us tenderly, specifically, benevolently, wisely, and eternally. Satan deceives us into thinking that our greatest comforts come from God's creation; the truth is that our greatest comfort comes from God himself.

Satan deceives us into thinking that receiving is better than giving; the truth is that giving is more blessed than receiving (see Acts 20:35). Satan deceives us into thinking that a "good" life avoids and evades trials, hardships, and suffering; the truth is that Christ called us to take up our cross daily (see Luke 9:23). His apostle taught us that we are strong when we are weak (see 2 Cor. 12:9), and our communion with the "man of sorrows" (Isa. 53:3) is rarely more profound than when our afflictions cause us to abandon all confidence in our own resources.

Indeed, according to the Scriptures, we are so deceived that we even confuse death and life. "There is a way that seems right to a man, but its end is the way to death" (Prov. 14:12). Satan attempts to make a way appear right and pleasant, when he knows it will destroy us. Thomas Brooks referred to this as Satan's great device, "to present the bait and hide the hook."[4]

Perhaps the greatest instrument of deception is cultural habit. Cultural anthropologists assure us that every culture establishes habits by which it shames some values or behaviors and honors others. Sociologists of knowledge similarly tell us that every culture, through its habits, creates "plausibility structures" by which some ideas and values appear more plausible and others less so. Since all cultures are now infected by human rebellion, all cultural activity has something of the Tower of Babel in it: an attempt to secure blessedness without God's re-inviting us to the garden from which we were banished.

Each of us is thus reared in a culture that regards as "normal" values and behaviors that might not at all accord with God's revealed norms.

---

4. Thomas Brooks, *Precious Remedies against Satan's Devices* (1652; repr., Edinburgh: Banner of Truth, 1984), 29.

And yet, the frequency with which we encounter cultural expressions may lull us into thinking that these expressions are "normal," when they are merely common in our culture. Some cultures revere those who are older, while our culture prizes youth—which accords more with the fifth commandment or with Solomon's proverbs? Some cultures are ascetic or communal, resisting the acquisition of material goods, while ours is capitalist and consumerist, encouraging the acquisition of material goods—which accords more with the teaching of Jesus? Some cultures respect their received traditions, eagerly studying the past, while ours values novelty, routinely assuming that "newer is better"—which is more consistent with the teaching of Scripture, which urges even new covenant saints, after the resurrection of Christ, to consider the faith of various old covenant saints (see Heb. 11)?

Diversion a special form of deception. Students of military history and tactics note that diversion is one of the most ancient military stratagems, a stratagem designed to turn the enemy's resources in a direction that will be less dangerous for the attacking force. Before Chancellorsville, for instance, Joe Hooker, knowing that Confederate spies had broken his flag-signal codes, sent a bogus signal that indicated a plan to attack the Shenandoah Valley, hoping thereby to dilute Robert E. Lee's forces by sending them westward. Similarly, before the D-Day invasion in June 1944, the Allied forces set up a false military base in the north of England, complete with plywood "tanks" and other matériel, in order to divert Hitler's gaze from Normandy. Those who wage war reckon that the next best thing to destroying an enemy's capacity to fight is *diverting* his military power to a place where it will be considerably less threatening.

Since the Enemy of all that is good does not always succeed at persuading us that good is evil and evil is good, he often blunts the force of God's kingdom by diverting its energies and resources. Indeed, he employed this tactic when he attempted to destroy Christ, the last Adam, in the temptation narrative of Matthew 4. Note, when Christ began to reestablish the reign of God through his public ministry, how Satan worked: by diversion. Satan could not take away Christ's power to work miracles, so he attempted to *divert* that power into such meaningless displays as turning stones to bread or leaping from the temple. Similarly, he offered the various kingdoms of the world, and their wealth, in exchange for Christ's worship. He was desperate to divert and deflect the powers of God's kingdom that were emerging in the person and work of Christ.

This attempt at diversion did not end with the incarnation of Christ. The church's temptation, historically, has resembled Christ's own temptation: to divert her energies from her principal tasks to those that are less significant. Quite frequently, the Enemy diverts the church's attention to some social reform movement, lest she devote her energies and resources to her distinctive concern for the spiritual and eternal wellbeing of her flock. He routinely diverts the church's intellectual energy from the vigorous study and refutation of particular cultural errors to quibbling and squabbling over theological issues that have little or no consequence, regardless of how they are resolved.[5] Often, he even succeeds in creating the same litigious atmosphere inside the church as exists outside it, which spends an enormous amount of time and energy adjudicating matters that are of comparatively little consequence. Obviously, he would rather have the church expend her resources fighting herself than fighting him, and the degree to which he has succeeded in thus diverting our energies would be admirable were it not so wicked.

This Diverter appears to take special delight in persuading ministers to use their pulpits to pursue their own peculiar hobby-horses (often faddish and culture-specific) rather than to declare the unchanging redemptive counsel of God. And few things please him more than cultivating in churchgoers a greater interest in "special" music, dramas, and entertainment than in the divinely instituted means of grace: prayer, the Word, and the sacraments.

5. See T. David Gordon, "Distractions from Orthodoxy," *Modern Reformation* 17, no. 5 (September/October 2008): 21–25.

Wouldn't it be nice if we could recognize that the means of grace are already "special"?

If I were the devil (no comments, please), and if I knew that "it pleased God through the folly of what we preach to save those who believe" (1 Cor. 1:21), I would do everything in my power to divert both the minister's and the congregation's attention and energy in any other direction to any other thing. I would suggest to ministers that what is "really" important is visitation, counseling, playing tennis with the youth, or administration; and I would suggest to worship committees that what is "really" important is giving people what they desire, amusing and entertaining them by abbreviated and simplistic preaching, or by diverting their senses to anything else but the preaching (e.g., the architecture, the interior design, the pipe organ, the choir, the choir robes, the praise band, the chorus, the dramatists, the jumbotron, and so on). If I were the devil, the very last thing I would want would be ministers like the apostles, who "devoted" themselves to prayer and to the ministry of the Word (see Acts 6:4). But then, I'm not the devil, so perhaps he is not doing such things to divert the church today.

Desires. In addition to deceit, Satan employs corrupt *desires* to attack us. In our fallen condition, having served the creature rather than the Creator, we have inverted the universe, prizing what God *made* more than the God who gave it. We have upside-down values and upside-down desires. "The desires of the flesh are against the Spirit, and the desires of the Spirit are against the flesh, for these are opposed to each other, to keep you from doing the things you want to do" (Gal. 5:17).

Further, these upside-down desires are often quite forceful (the Puritans frequently called them "violent"), and when they are unusually forceful, they are called "passions." These strong desires overwhelm our reason, causing us to behave stupidly.[6] Some pas-

6. Thus, they are studied by behavioral economists, such as Daniel Ariely, the James B. Duke Professor of Psychology and Behavioral Economics at Duke University. See his *Predictably Irrational: The Hidden Forces that Shape Our Decisions*

sions are so strong that, once ignited, they almost sweep us away. The unbelieving world thinks of such passions as "irresistible"— and indeed, apart from God's grace, they genuinely are irresistible.

What causes quarrels and what causes fights among you? Is it not this, that your passions are at war within you? You desire and do not have, so you murder. You covet and cannot obtain, so you fight and quarrel. (James 4:1–2)

Beloved, I urge you as sojourners and exiles to abstain from the passions of the flesh, which wage war against your soul. (1 Peter 2:11)

Our Weapons: Faith and Repentance
The weapons of the Christian church are manifold and, we trust, growing. One can only hope and pray that "research and development" will never end, as long as the church is militant. But among the church's foremost weapons are faith and repentance—these are the antidotes, respectively, to deception and desire. Faith assents to (and rests in) what God reveals, and the more our minds are influenced by his revelation, the less easy it is for the Evil One to deceive us. The ignorant and the uncertain are much easier to deceive than the thoughtful, the learned, and the well-grounded. Those whose faith is fortified by many hours of study, reflection, meditation, instruction, and conversation are more resistant to deception than those whose faith is shaped by sloganized or emotional Christianity. Similarly,

---

(New York: HarperCollins, 2008), especially chapter 5, "The Influence of Arousal," 89–105. See also Nicholas Carr, "Is Google Making Us Stupid?" *The Atlantic* 302, no. 1 (July/August, 2008): 56–63; Mark Bauerlein, *The Dumbest Generation: How the Digital Age Stupefies Young Americans and Jeopardizes Our Future* (New York: Tarcher Press, 2008); Ori Brafman and Rom Brafman, *Sway: The Irresistible Pull of Irrational Behavior* (New York: Doubleday, 2008); and Farhad Manjoo, *True Enough: Learning to Live in a Post-Fact Society* (Hoboken, NJ: Wiley & Sons, 2008). I fully expect a new area of academic studies to emerge: "Stupid Studies." In fact, behavioral economics is very close to being such a discipline.

repentance is perhaps the greatest antidote to sinful desire—it is the deliberate, intentional determination to exercise self-control and self-denial regarding some specific thought, attitude, or behavior. Indeed, it is the very repudiation of such desire.

When one considers how effectively these two weapons oppose Satan's primary tactics, it is not surprising to notice how frequently the two are spoken of together in the New Testament.

> Now after John was arrested, Jesus came into Galilee, proclaiming the gospel of God, and saying, "The time is fulfilled, and the kingdom of God is at hand; *repent* and *believe* in the gospel." (Mark 1:14–15)

> How I did not shrink from declaring to you anything that was profitable, and teaching you in public and from house to house, testifying both to Jews and to Greeks of *repentance* toward God and of *faith* in our Lord Jesus Christ. (Acts 20:20–21)

> Therefore let us leave the elementary doctrine of Christ and go on to maturity, not laying again a foundation of *repentance* from dead works and of *faith* toward God. (Heb. 6:1)

The two great weapons in the believer's arsenal are faith and repentance. Each of these is well-suited to counterattack deceit and desire. The "solution" to Satan's deceptions is to believe what God has revealed. The "solution" to evil desires is to repent of them (the sooner, the better). Faith and repentance, then, are like a soldier's two legs: with one we stride toward God, and with the other we stride away from sin.

Faith is the positive side of the coin, if you will. On the opposite side is repentance. Faith treasures what is right and true and trusts in what God has said, relying entirely on his Word. True faith is not mere assent, but a heartfelt trust in God's revelation, because the faithful one reveres God as loving and wise. True repentance is not mere resolve but a resolve based on the perception of sin's blackness and deadliness. To repent requires a genuine, soul-felt acknowledgment of how vile and wicked sin is.

Application of the Warfare Model

The warfare model reminds us that the stakes of our decision-making are high. In a sense, every decision makes the next battle easier or harder; every decision either strengthens or weakens us amid life's greater battle. As we evaluate our past decisions, and as we consider making present and future ones, the warfare model demands a broader field of vision—it suggests that we look beyond the immediate consequences of our decisions to the longer-range consequences and tendencies to which they may lead. Especially, perhaps, it challenges us to think strategically: to think of all of life as having both an "offensive" and a "defensive" component. Offensively, we desire to take new ground not previously occupied; defensively, we desire to protect hard-fought ground from the Evil One.

To illustrate this, imagine two individuals, Mary and Bill. Mary participates in a wide range of church and community activities and is a devoted (and busy!) wife and mother. Bill is single, contemplative, somewhat reclusive. Mary's faith is fervent and sincere, but her schedule is so full that there is little time in her life for prayer, thoughtful study, or meditation. Bill is similarly sincere, but his personality has left him comparatively withdrawn, if not aloof, from others.

Both Mary and Bill attend First Lutheran Church, and the consistory has announced a new program for distributing goods to those in the congregation who are needy. It asks if anyone in the church is willing to chair this project, and both Mary and Bill think about it. What should they do? Well, Mary is busy enough (probably too busy), and at this point in her life, it would be poor strategy to assume yet another responsibility. Bill, however, needs precisely to actively serve his neighbor, and the fact that he has no family responsibilities means that he has more than enough time to do this. Further, such service would help him to develop in areas where he is comparatively underdeveloped—that is, to take new ground from the Enemy.

Thus, when they face this decision *strategically*, two different individuals might legitimately give two different answers to the same question (Mary declines; Bill accepts). While the Scriptures do not say to all people, "Thou shalt never serve as chairman of any form of church ministry," and while they do not say to all people, "Thou shalt always serve as chairman of every church ministry," the warfare model brings light to the matter that other models do not. For Mary, this is not a strategic time to increase her activity; if anything, she needs more time for the contemplative aspects of the Christian life. But for Bill, this is a strategic time for him to actively serve others and to thereby emulate our serving Lord.

Similarly, the decision regarding which local church to attend is fraught with strategic considerations and consequences. When a family elects to attend and support one local church (and therefore *not* to attend and support the other local options), this has profound consequences for both the family and the local churches. Ideally, our affiliation with a local church would be highly beneficial both to us and to the church—an affiliation through which we can both bless and be blessed, both serve and be served. Of course, we will rarely achieve such a perfect blend. At some moments in our pilgrimage, we may need to be served more than to serve, and vice versa. In some circumstances, the decision to attend a smaller, struggling church or church plant will demand more of us, but will do more good, strategically, for the kingdom of God than would attending a larger, better-established church. In other circumstances, the opposite could true. Thinking strategically, then, about self, family, and the local and universal kingdom of God might lead two different families to make two different decisions, both of which might be "right."

Such examples also demonstrate how the five models inform one another. In some sense, the strategic question of which ministry to perform or which local church to attend is also a matter of wisdom, and it is certainly a matter that affects communion with God. While any legitimate form of service in any legitimate expression of the visible church is lawful and is an occasion to imitate God, not every decision is equally wise, not every decision has the same consequences for our communion with God and with other saints, and, surely, not every decision has the same consequences for the warfare between the seed of the Serpent and the Seed of the woman.

Questions for Discussion and Reflection

1. Name five of Satan's designs.
2. How does the understanding of all of life as warfare challenge or convict you in your decision-making?
3. How might the warfare model encourage us to boldly apply other models, such as the law model, at times when doing so might be uncomfortable in our secular culture?
4. How might the communion model help you to resist the Enemy's weapons of deceit and desire?
5. In what way does the warfare model have implications for every decision we make?

Case Study

Return to your case study from the opening chapter and answer the following questions with it in mind.

1. What is helpful about viewing the situation through a warfare lens?
2. What aspects of the situation, if any, does the warfare model not seem to address?
3. Based on the warfare model, what decision(s) would you advise a person in this situation to make? Why?
4. Are you satisfied with how the warfare model addresses this situation? Why or why not?

CONCLUSIONS

The purpose of this brief study has been to encourage a broader vision of ethics or decision-making, one that is informed by the Holy Scriptures and the Christian tradition. Different traditions within the Christian church have tended to benefit more from some of our five models than from others, and the goal of my study has been to encourage the entire church to benefit from the insights of these various traditions. Especially, the goal of this study has been to encourage decision-making that is more comprehensively informed by the rich teaching of Holy Scripture.

A broader ethical vision could not only contribute to a healthy ecumenism but also protect us from the potentially limited vision of our own tradition. I remain persuaded, as a member of a law-model-dominant tradition, that some of our tendency toward argumentativeness and angularity is due to our related tendency to perceive decision-making exclusively in terms of obedience and disobedience. We are less well-versed in thinking of decisions in terms of wisdom, strategy, or the imitation of God. On the other hand, those reared in more pietistic traditions, traditions that have been shaped primarily by the communion model, may benefit from the kind of precise ethical reasoning reflected in the Westminster Larger Catechism's exposition of the Decalogue. Imagine the kind of reasoning that led the Westminster Assembly to list as one of the sins of the ninth commandment "speaking the truth unseasonably."[1] I'm not sure I could name three individuals I've met who have ever *considered* the possibility that speaking the truth "unseasonably" might be a sin, though, having thought about it through the years, I have come to appreciate Westminster's opinion on the matter and have often wished that others would observe it.

While it wasn't my purpose to argue for a hierarchy among the models in this work, it is probably not inappropriate to state candidly that I consider the heart, or essence, of our ethical reasoning to reside in the imitation model. We humans, by essence, are *imago Dei*, and our duty, corresponding to that essence, is *imitatio Dei*. God orders and rules all things, and he expects us to submit to and obey that rule (law model); God creates and governs the world wisely, and we are to conduct ourselves wisely (wisdom model); God wages war against destructive rebellion, and we are to join that warfare (warfare model); God exists everlastingly in Trinitarian communion, and he enables us to commune with him and with others (communion model).

Therefore, while each of the five models contributes its own perspective to ethical decision-making and thus merits consideration, the imitation model remains the intellectual, philosophical, and theological basis of the entire ethical enterprise, and it actually comprehends the other four models within itself.[2] Consequently, students of a biblical *theology* of ethics would rightly structure their thinking by that model. Further, as a practical matter, the imitation model not only provides more insight than any of the others but also motivates those who know the right but find it hard to do. When we recall Christ's saying "Come to me, all who labor" (Matt. 11:28), we find ourselves desiring to be more welcoming and redemptive toward others. When we consider the great humiliation of his incarnation (see Phil. 2:1–11), we find ourselves contented, even privileged, to

---

1. Westminster Larger Catechism, answer 145.
2. In philosophical terms, ethics is grounded in metaphysics and anthropology. What the human truly and really *is* dictates what the human rightly ought to *do*.

perform the lowliest acts of service.[3] When we remember that he loved us while we were yet his enemies (see Rom. 5:8), we find ourselves wishing to treat compassionately and forgivingly those who have injured us. When we recall again that though he was rich, he become poor for our sakes (see 2 Cor. 8:9), we find ourselves eager to perform small (and sometimes large) acts of charity.

In another place and time, then, I would like to have written a biblical *theology* of ethics, in which the emphases would have been slightly different from those in this work. But I hope it will have been useful to have placed this small book before a thoughtful Christian public as it is, and that some of that public will have found it helpful in the task of thinking Christianly about decision-making. As a minister of the gospel, I would remind my readership that the "work of God" is to believe in the One whom he sent (John 6:29). I would rather that all my readers believe in Christ and live badly than not believe in Christ and live well.

---

3. In Anna L. Waring's lovely language, "Content to fill a little space, if Thou be glorified." See "Father, I Know That All My Life," 1850.

Did you find this book helpful?
Consider writing a review online.
We appreciate your feedback!

Or write to P&R at editorial@prpbooks.com
with your comments. We'd love to hear from you.